THE LOVELY WORLD OF RICHI-SAN

THE LOVELY

BY ALLAN R. BOSWORTH

HARPER & ROW,

WORLD OF RICHI-SAN

PUBLISHERS, NEW YORK

This book is dedicated, with affection and respect, to Bess Good, and Admiral Roscoe Good, U.S. Navy (Retired). They left, in Japan, a job well done, and friendships as enduring as the sea that will forever link Richi-san's lovely world with ours.

FOREWORD

TWICE IN A CENTURY, FOR BETTER OR FOR WORSE, AMERICA TURNED
the world of Japan sakasama—upside down.

The first time was in 1853, when the "Black Ships" of the United
States Navy anchored off Kurihama, and Commodore Matthew
Calbraith Perry negotiated a treaty—somewhat at gun point—that
ended Japan's seclusion and brought about the most amazing industrial revolution the world has ever seen.

The second time was in 1945, when forces under General Doug-
las MacArthur landed at Yokohama to begin an Occupation unique
in history, and to bring reforms and the seeds of democracy.

Sentimentalists have wept over the coming of both, although each
was inevitable. Each contributed—Perry more than MacArthur—to
the destruction of a way of life we shall never see again. It was an
anachronistic way of life; it had miserable and cruel and shameful
sides, and faced ultimate doom. But it had a classic beauty that was
old when America was still peopled by savages. It was a life scaled
in miniature and lived with the precise, clear-cut exactness of a
cameo, and it was well suited to people dwelling in a small, crowded
country. The Japanese have always excelled in miniatures—in tiny
gardens, in poems of seventeen syllables, in the manufacture of
toys, in art expressed by spare strokes of the brush. The cesspools

of the old days sometimes mirrored temples of an ancient faith; and if feudal corruption and injustice existed, there remained the shining feudal virtues of loyalty and courage and sacrifice. The ties of family and clan were commendably strong; devotion to the Emperor was not, in itself, a bad thing, any more than an American's devotion to our Flag is bad. It has been said that all of us live by signs and symbols, more than we know.

All that follows here had its real beginnings with Perry and MacArthur, because every American who goes to Japan must wear their mantles. Their moments at Kurihama and Yokohama were the significant meetings of East and West. In this book, I shall relate another and humbler meeting of the two. It is not historical, but neither is it—as the others were—impersonal.

Richi-san and the other members of the Asano family may and may not be "typical," although I should like to think that there are millions of Japanese like them. They are honest and kind, hardworking and true, and their humility in no way affects their natural pride. They are far more religious than the average American family, and the precepts of their Nichiren Buddhist faith do not differ greatly from the teachings of Christianity. Their politeness is an inherent trait, born of a thousand years of culture and breeding, and they are, instinctively, gentlefolk.

I taught them most of the English they know, during two tours of Navy duty that gave me almost six years in Japan, but I am not a teacher, and the language barrier was always difficult. From me, they learned the word "war," and in a way I am sorry for that. Before I taught them that word, they spoke of World War Two as "*fire* between States and Japan."

There may be an important truth in this, going beyond mere semantics. Fires may be started by incendiarists, but they are never started by the entire people of any nation. Sometimes they are caused by carelessness, or by internal combustion.

Allan R. Bosworth

THE LOVELY WORLD OF RICHI-SAN

ONE

THIS WAS THE ENEMY

AT DAWN IN TOKYO BAY, THE SEA CHANGED COLOR, AND MORNING put on a different smell. There is always romance in arrival at far places: March wind spilled the day's first hesitant light into the phantom sails of curiously rigged fishing craft, and green hills abeam were bordered by clusters of tiny, tile-topped houses huddling along winding ways. But the sea no longer had the clean beauty of deep and swinging salt water. It lay flat and sluggish under the offshore wind; it took on the bilious tint of channel and shoal and lazy tidal river, and now it floated the noisome refuse of man—the only creature powerful enough and careless enough to sully the sea. The gusty wind brought a variety of smells, but could not blend them any more successfully than the sea could disguise the discard of the populated shore. It carried in turn the stink of emptying sewers and the primordial salty rankness of tideflats where billions of tiny creatures had died overnight; it hinted at the fishbait and pitch and hemp smells of all waterfronts, and the black suffocative breath of factories farther on. And then it brought the signature smell of the Far East—the *man* smell, the sweetish, unmistakable odor of crowded humanity. This is noticeable only when you first arrive, or after you have been away. It is a cloying and clinging smell which sometimes permeates clothing long unpacked, and once known will not be forgotten.

The wind carried lovely things, too, but they were drowned. On it were the renewed promise of green things growing taller, and the good smell of rich earth turned over to feel the warmth of another sun. The wind ran along the slopes of the green hills, above the doll-houses, where flowering plum trees made a fringe of white lace, their scent too subtle to survive, their loveliness too delicate to linger on the crowded senses. There was beauty ashore for the finding, but it was not on the crowded doorstep of Japan. . . .

Millions of Americans have come this way before now, most of them in the big gray Navy transports that nudged the Yokohama docks. They came first in the wasteful wake of war, to police the land, to stride tall down the Tokyo Ginza, or to spill out into camps from Hokkaido to Kyushu; they came later, in a hurry and in ever-increasing numbers, to be shuttled across a farther sea to fight another war. Too many of them died on the tomb-pocked ridges of Korea, where it is always too hot or too cold, too muddy or too dusty; or they fell in the stinking rice paddies of that same unhappy land. The lucky lived. They soldiered well, and accumulated points toward the day when they could return, briefly, to the green and flowering islands of Japan—to the neon-lighted world capital of Tokyo—for the "Little R" of rest and rehabilitation.

They dreamed of this in Korea, when there was time to dream, and they did not always dream of America, because America was too far away. Sometimes America was a beloved face carried in a wallet window. The plastic got rubbed, the face was a little blurred. America was a letter to be read again before the lights went out, before sunset faded over a foxhole. It was a blessed, faraway place where you never saw belly hunger in a kid's eyes. It was where everybody had big cars, and there were good roads for driving. It was known by various names: CONUS, the Big Island. Uncle Sugar, "Z.I."—the Zone of the Interior. The Land of the Big PX.

But it was a million miles and eighteen months away. Meanwhile, there was Japan. . . .

JAPAN HAS BEEN STRANGER, ENEMY AND FRIEND. IT IS A BEAUTIFUL place, a tragic and haunted place, and it is far away. It seems a long time since I first went there, although it has been only seven years, and the memories are both fresh and elusive. Japan is ancient and modern, happy and sad: it is the roaring bedlam of Tokyo at the rush hour, and the haunting, sad-sweet cry of a noodle flute along the dark alleyways at midnight, when all the little houses are shuttered and sleeping, and the tile roofs weep with the quiet sorrow of the rain. Japan is as gay as a Gion kimono, and as lighthearted as the laughter of children; it is a country where the very young and the very old are loved and cherished—and yet there will always be other children crying in their sleep with hunger, and elders who

throw themselves in front of speeding trains. Not many will hear of these individual tragedies, because the face Japan wears for the stranger is as unrevealing as the traditional masks of the Noh plays, or the thick powdered make-up of the geisha. Behind these, the Japanese people are sensitive and highly emotional, easily moved to tears or laughter. Signs and symbols, the stars and the seasons, are important to them. During the maples' flaming, or April's brief blossoming of the cherry trees, or the waxing of a full moon, they can get drunk on beauty alone. . . .

When I came to Japan the first time, the Korean War was being prosecuted in the limited fashion allowed to that "police action," and the Occupation was in its last months. The Navy transport moved up to the Yokohama pier, and I looked down upon a curious scene. Scores of American husbands were waiting—after fourteen months or longer—for their wives and children. They stood in a prescribed space, the more senior officers quite naturally moving into the more advantageous front ranks. Each clutched a small floral offering. In their eager anticipation they weaved back and forth and strained sidewise in the effort to catch the first glimpse of a beloved face at the transport rail. This movement became more pronounced as the ship went through the business of tying up; it took on a pattern, a rhythm; it came near being a ballet. They danced, flowers in hand, while an Army band drowned out the shouts of "Hello, darling!" and "Welcome to Japan!" and "Look, there's Daddy! No, not there —over *there!*"

Nobody was meeting me, except two officers I had never seen, come to escort me to my new office and a strange job in Tokyo. I turned away from the consciously tender scene, and studied the porters and customs officials on the pier—the Japanese. And it occurred to me suddenly that these people—these energetic, active, bowing and smiling people—had lately been the Enemy. . . .

I REALLY KNEW NOTHING ABOUT THEM. OH, I HAD KNOWN THEM in the South Pacific during the war, but not very well; my war was not the kind in which one came to grips, hand to hand, with the foe. The only Japanese I felt I had ever really known was in San Francisco, back in the latter thirties. He did not know me. He was a lieutenant commander in the Imperial Japanese Navy, and a spy in the United States. I was a newspaperman, and an inactive Naval Reserve officer in Intelligence, and an eager beaver. I was frequently called upon to keep a sharp surveillance on Lieutenant Commander Watanabe during my leisure time. When the lights went out in his California Street apartment and he emerged with the cute little Hawaiian-born nisei girl who went with his job, I also emerged from the apartment Naval Intelligence had rented just across the street. Wearing a snap-brim hat and a reasonable facsimile of a trench coat, I followed them along Post and Fillmore Streets in the Japanese quarter. It was very easy to follow them, because the little nisei girl was built like a Shetland pony, with a derrière that stood out, twinkling, in any teeming thoroughfare.

Not that either Watanabe or the Navy ever learned anything of importance. He and the girl would make their appointed rounds of fish and sake stores, then return to the apartment and go to bed before dinner. Later, when we wired his apartment for sound, we confirmed this program, and we followed him closely enough (finally, we stole all his gear) to know that he took nothing important back to Japan with him. He was relieved by another Japanese agent, who inherited the little nisei girl, and the Navy set about watching *him*. But Watanabe got nothing. He was not smart, and he was selling his country short.

I had only contempt for Lieutenant Commander Watanabe; I would have respected him if he had been dangerous and clever. I had hated the Japanese, during the war, with a hot and patriotic hate. And now I was arriving in Japan, almost seven years after the war, with mixed feelings. Japan was soon to be a sovereign nation. We were supposed to be friends with the Japanese people.

The two officers met me, and took me to my new office in the Rice Exchange Hotel in Tokyo. For a couple of weeks, I saw nothing to make me change my mind about the Japanese. They were quaint and polite and energetic. They had been the Enemy. They were willing and neat and eager to please, but they had been the Enemy, and nobody could tell what they were thinking.

And then, through purely fortuitous circumstances, I met Goto-san and the Many Cousins, and the other members of the Asano family. . . .

GOTO-SAN HAD SET UP SHOP AS A SPARE-TIME ARTIST ON THE GINZA, working there during the evening hours. I walked that way and encountered him, a young man, wiry and lean and smiling. He spoke almost no English, but he did a quick sketch of me that was good. I saw him again one evening as I left the office, and he saw my Jaguar sports car and all but prostrated himself before it in utter adoration. Driving an automobile, I found later, was his regular job. His worship of the car was so complete that I would have been most unkind if I had not offered him a ride one evening. We left the Ginza, which is the Broadway of Tokyo, and he directed me migi to hidari (left and right) through the formidable traffic, and told me in Japanese, in broken English, and by signs, that having once ridden in that car he would be happy to die immediately. Once he had me stop while he telephoned. Finally, we came to a modestly poor section in northern Tokyo, which I identified on my map as Takinogawa. We parked the car in a walled enclosure, listening to frogs chortling nearby, and Goto-san led me to the entrance of a ground floor apato, or apartment. Inside were the buzz of conversation and sounds of laughter.

We removed our shoes and stepped on the polished wooden floor of the hallway. A voice called, softly, "Yoku irasshaimashita!" which was to say we had arrived and were welcome. A slender, pretty girl who appeared to be about seventeen knelt gracefully to open the sliding paper door, and we were shown into a room where perhaps a dozen people sat. They were all smiling. They did not rise to greet us—it is not proper to rise when wearing kimono—but the women came to their knees, placed their hands palms down before them, and bowed so low their foreheads touched the tatami mats. Everybody murmured a lengthier greeting.

"Good evening," I said, and bowed awkwardly in return.

"Konnichi-wa!" they said, and indicated a cushion in the place of honor before the tokonoma, or ceremonial alcove, which contained a simple flower arrangement. I sat down, cross-legged and self-conscious. There was a moment of bashful silence, then some polite but irrepressible hand-over-mouth giggles. I laughed. Everybody laughed, uproariously.

"I am sorry," I said. "I cannot speak Japanese." I put on my glasses, and found the equivalent phrase in the Conversation Dictionary. "Nihon-go hanasu dekimasen," I said.

This was a poor effort, a broken phrase, but it brought nods and smiles and more giggles. One of the young men addressed me in Japanese, finishing with a bow and a smile. Then the pretty young girl looked at me and spoke English. It was broken, but melodious as a flute.

"Oji Cousin verree sorree he cannot Engrish. If can Engrish, Oji Cousin too muchee happee. He said."

All the others looked at her with family pride and affection. *She* could Engrish. Then Goto-san spoke, and she translated.

"Goto-san su-peaking sank you verree muchee, kindly to him. He said."

I told her that her English was very good, and that I only wished I could speak Japanese as well. She blushed, and poured me a cup of tea. Every movement of her hands was as delicately graceful as the sweep of a sea gull's wing.

"Oh, I don' sink so!" She laughed. "Sank you verree muchee, but I don' sink so! Cannot good Engrish—I'm verree bad head!"

I did not realize it at that moment, but I had just met Richi-san and some of the Many Cousins of the Asano family. I had found a number of gaido (guides) far superior to the hired, professional variety. The fact that I owned a car, and they did not, gave matters a curious twist. During the next several years I would show them their own country by taking them to places they had never seen, and they would interpret Japan and things Japanese to me. . . .

Out of that first unplanned meeting came weekly gatherings, and I found myself teaching an informal class in Conversational English. Also, I had a title. It was "Papa-san," a slang term, not without affection and respect, given to the boss or manager of any project. My students were all Asanos—there were dozens of cousins and a number of aunts and uncles living all over Tokyo, usually introduced to me by residence place names. These included Kyobashi Cousin, Oji Cousin, Shinagawa Cousin and Shinjuku Aunt and Unc', but I also met Next Door Wife-san—the lady who lived next door. And then, to make things utterly confusing for a while, there was Next Door Pretty Soon Wife-san. This title turned out to be logical enough: it meant that the lady lived only a little way— pretty soon—from next door. At that time Richi-san's father and mother, who were known as O-jii-chan and O-baa-chan, or Honorable Little Grandfather and Honorable Little Grandmother, were living in the Asanos' "home countree," at Shizukawa. Life was full of surprises, because Richi-san said her baby was living with them —and it developed that she was a widow, nearly twice as old as the seventeen she looked.

"My baby, Papa-san, will soon being old enough for student [school], and I must bringing her to the Tokyo. But ever' time I'm su-peaking bringing her to the Tokyo, my fazzer and-a muzzer too muchee cry-cry. So what you gonna doing? I *cannot* bringing her to the Tokyo."

THE ENGLISH CLASSES STARTED GRADUALLY. EVERYBODY ACQUIRED a bilingual dictionary and gave it much thumbing. English words were laboriously spelled out in notebooks, and I had just as difficult a time with their Japanese equivalents. Nobody was making notable progress, except Richi-san, who apparently had an ear for language and seldom forgot a word once its meaning had been explained. She enjoyed listening to the speech of Americans; she frequently tuned in broadcasts on the Far East Network of the Armed Forces Radio Service, and would ask me later about phrases she remembered.

"Papa-san, what means 'This is verree in-ter-*est*-ing'?"

And when I told her she would nod gravely. "Ah, so! *Now* I understand. Verree in-ter-*est*-ing!"

At first she had great difficulty with "l" sounds, as do most Japanese, although she used some of them unconsciously. There is no "l" in the Japanese Roman arufabetto, and "r" is always substituted for it. The other Many Cousins found "l" even more difficult, and when we put aside the dictionaries and had Honorable Tea and a session of singing, the difficulty was delightfully noticeable:

> You are my shunshine,*
> My onry shunshine;
> You make me hoppee
> When su-kies are gu-ray;
> You neva know, dear,
> How muchee I rove you—
> Prease don't take my shunshine away!

Or another Stateside song that was then very popular among members of the American Security Forces and their Japanese hosts:

> I was danshing, with my darring,
> To the Tenneshee wartz,
> When an old friend-o I hoppened to shee . . .

"Hold it!" I would cry. "Wait a minute. Not 'wartz'—waltz! Not 'darring'—dar-*ul*-ing!"

"Ah, so, Papa-san! Verree sorree—more better next time. Papa-san, you 'ant more koppu tea?"

We sang Japanese songs, too, and it must be admitted that Papa-san made just as many mistakes in pronunciation as his pupils did, to say nothing of a congenital inability to carry a tune in a basket:

> Sho, sho, sho-jo-ji,*
> Sho-jo-ji no ni-wa-wa,
> Tsun, tsun, tsu-ki-yo-da,
> Minadete koi koi koi!
> Oirano tomodachi,
> Pon po-ko-pon no pon!

* See copyright page.

Makeru-na, makeru-na,
O shosan-ni makeru-na,
Koi, koi, koi, koi, koi, koi—
Minadete koi koi koi!

This is the song of Tanuki-san, the badger, which Eartha Kitt later made somewhat famous in America, except that she substituted, "I'm so hungry, I'm so hungry!" for "Makeru-na, makeru-na!" There is nothing about hunger in the original Japanese. The song says it is a fine moonlight night, and Tanuki-san, beating his belly like a drum, calls on all his friends to come out and enjoy it. . . .

THE WAY IN WHICH RICHI-SAN FINALLY MASTERED HER "L" SOUNDS was simple, indeed: she only needed to be shown that she had been pronouncing "l" all along, unconsciously. One evening I noticed a single flower in the vase that stood in the tokonoma.

"Richi-san," I asked, "what is the Japanese name for that pretty flower?"

"Oh, I'm forget, Papa-san. Verree ba-ad head!"

"Well, I have forgotten the English word, too. It's not really an English word, perhaps. Maybe more like Latin."

"That kind frower having in States, Papa-san?"

"Oh, yes—in California, we have many of that kind."

A moment of concentration, then, "Oh, now I remember, Papa-san! We calling that kind frower 'gladiolus.' "

I chuckled. "Yes, and we call it gladiolus, too. But tell me—if you can say 'gladiolus,' why can't you say 'flower'—not 'frower'?"

"Oh, different, Papa-san! Bee-cause, gladiolus we always have!"

Richi-san had come to Tokyo to get a job, and had been working as a kohi (coffee) girl in a large Japanese restaurant. The hours were uncertainly long, and she had to stay on her feet all the time. She was small and frail, and when she had a chest X ray the doctor told her she was in danger of contracting tuberculosis. After that she made kimono for sale, walked daily in the open air, and got more rest. Her father, who was still in her "countree," helped her financially, and her health improved.

TWO

ENGRISH AS IT WAS NEVER
SPOKEN BEE-FORE

IT MUST BE ADMITTED THAT I, AS PAPA-SAN, HAD BEEN WOEFULLY miscast in the role of teacher, and therefore the English Conversation Class, which ran for about eight months, was alternately played as comedy and mystery, and sometimes with elements of both. We gathered at Goto-san's apato twice weekly, except on occasions when Navy duties took me to the Peace Tent at Panmunjom, in Korea, where a ceaseless Communist harangue was blocking armistice negotiations; or to the Seventh Fleet task force off Wonsan, where the air was still loud with round-the-clock carrier strikes. When I went on these missions, the Many Cousins were much concerned, and it was difficult to convince them that I was fighting a swivel-chair kind of war. Richi-san, the interpreter and spokesman, would say, "Be careful, Papa-san. We will pu-raying Buddha." It was always an occasion for celebration when I returned to drink another koppu tea, eat home-cooked sukiyaki, and conduct another class.

I was not learning much Japanese. The nouns, yes—I could pick up the nouns. I could look them up in my Japanese dictionary, and stop at a sidewalk fruit shop and utter the word *kaki*, which means persimmons. The trouble is that kaki also means oysters, unless it is spoken with a difference so faint as to be almost indistinguishable to the American ear, and the fruit shop proprietor might look blank and say "Arimasen," meaning that he had no oysters. To make it even more confusing, kaki is also the word for flowering plants, the flowering season, firearms, heat, summertime, and a fence. The Japanese language is full of such homonyms, extremely confusing to the foreigner. Of course, the Japanese do not utter a single word out of a dictionary—the phrases or sentences they speak make the meaning clear through word association.

Every schoolboy in Japan, however, must learn to read and write the equivalent of three languages. First is the Chinese-Japanese ideographic script, called kanji, which initially looks like so much hen scratching to Occidental eyes, and requires the student to learn to recognize some two thousand characters at sight. (In kanji, the meanings of words which sound exactly alike become unmistakably clear: nobody could confuse oysters with persimmons or fences.) Next, the student must learn kana. This is a syllabary of fifty sounds, and may be written in katakana, which is like printed letters, or in hiragana, which is more like script. An American who applies himself can at least learn katakana. Any Japanese word can be written in it, in less time than we could write the word in long-hand, and it is necessary and useful to the Japanese because the ancient kanji does not include any of the many borrowed foreign words or any technical or scientific terms. My own name cannot be expressed in kanji—perhaps the ideograph coming nearest to it is one pronounced "basu" (the "a" like "ah") and meaning "palm tree nut." But while it takes eight characters to spell Bosworth in English, katakana can handle it in five sounds which come out "Ba-su-wo-ru-tu." It could be done similarly in hiragana, but the script is more difficult, just as it is more difficult to learn writing a round schoolboy hand than it is to print in Roman letters.

Finally, the Japanese pupil has to master those Roman letters. This is romaji, and consists of our alphabet minus the letters l, q, v and x. "Love" is a borrowed English word that comes out rabu in romaji, and "rendezvous" is a neat randebu, just as "television" becomes terebi. A letter written in romaji could lead to confusion, because of the homonyms—oysters, persimmons, and all those other things listed earlier would be spelled kaki.

By the time a Japanese boy is in high school or college he has developed a very considerable ability to concentrate. In fact, he's usually smart as a whip, and I think he could learn English much faster than I could learn Japanese. . . .

IT WAS THE CONSTRUCTION THAT GAVE ME THE MOST TROUBLE. IT isn't easy to learn to ask "May I smoke?" when what you are saying, literally, is "Tobacco drinking even all right is it?" (There is another word which means "smoking," but nonde, in "Tabako wo nonde mo ii desuka?" means "drinking," apparently in the sense of "gulping." (As a pipe addict, I gulp smoke.) "May I have a glass of water?" comes out "Water one glass wish to receive, the thing is."

Besides, not all the nouns and phrases I learned were of any use to me in ordinary conversation. One summer evening when I went to the apato, the class was already assembled, and I could see them through the large, open window, from the alley. I removed my boots there, sat on the window sill, and swung my legs inside, instead of going around to the front door. A few seconds later, a woman began screaming in the house just across the alley. I scrambled back through the window in time to catch sight of a man fleeing down the narrow, dimly lighted street, and gave chase without bothering about my boots. He turned the corner, and was soon lost in the maze of dark alleys. When I came back, I asked Richi-san what had happened.

"Hentai, Papa-san!" she said. "Ba-ad man!"

The woman who had screamed was now taking down her wash from the bamboo pole which Japanese housewives use for a clothes-line, and Richi-san made me understand that the man had stolen a slip and other lingerie.

"Oh," I said. "He will sell the clothes?"

"Not selling to clothes!" she said emphatically. "Hentai!"

I thought the word perhaps meant thief, and looked in the dictionary. Hentai was a formation, such as a formation of airplanes, and that didn't do any good. But just below was the same romanized word, defined as "an anomaly; abnormality (abnormal mentality)."

"Ah, so?" I said. "Maybe crazy?"

"Maybe like crazy," Richi-san said. (She pronounced it ku-razy.) And I had learned another unusual word, under unusual circumstances. But it was not one I could use.

Next to the difficulties of construction were those of learning to count. I had never really realized that in the English language we have many collective nouns which vary according to what is being counted: a team of horses, a span of mules, a brace of pheasants, a pair of shoes, and so on. (If you want to carry it to seldom-used extremes, we have a pride of lions, a gaggle of geese, a rasher of bacon, a clutch of eggs, and things like that.) But the Japanese have gone us one better. The words for counting, in Japan, vary according to the type and shape of things being counted. Eight persons are hachi-nin, eight animals are hatto, eight birds become hachi-wa, and eight packages, or bundles, are called ya-tsutsumi. This sort of thing goes on through flat objects, such as sheets of paper, cylindrical objects, round objects, and long objects. Fortunately, after you have passed the number of ten, you usually speak the name of the thing and then the simple numeral. Many times I have bought ten or fifteen apples when I wanted only six; it was easier that way. . . .

THE ENGLISH CONVERSATION CLASS, EVEN UNDER AN INCOMPETENT teacher, could have been better organized. There was no formal course of study; the meetings became more social than educational. I taught Richi-san and some of the others how to play dominoes, and they began introducing me to the more exotic forms of Japanese food, and were delighted when I liked it. Not all of the Many Cousins could attend every meeting. Goto-san had taken a job as a takushi-cab driver, and was literally jockeying his cab about the streets of Tokyo eighteen hours a day until his energy won him promotion, and he was put to driving a bus operated by the same transportation company. Goto-san had to drop out of the classes, but his pretty wife, Yoshii-san, was always at the apato when we gathered there. It was a rather long way for Kyobashi Cousin to come, and even farther for Shinjuku Aunt and Unc', but each of these usually showed up once a week.

Shinjuku Aunt must have been very nearly sixty. She usually wore kimono, in preference to Western-style dress, and her long hair was still done in the traditional style now most often seen only on geisha. Her husband, Shinjuku Unc', a baldheaded man, small and neat and quiet, had been retired for some years from the import-export business. Sometimes they brought their youngest daughter, the girl Richi-san introduced to me as "Small Cousin." Her name was Takiko, but Small Cousin she remained. In Western clothes, Small Cousin could easily have been taken for Spanish or French, and she was so beautiful she made heads turn on the Ginza, where one sees many pretty girls.

All of them, including Oji Cousin and his wife—they lived only about a mile away—looked to Richi-san to play the spokesman and interpreter, and she never missed a class. Nor was she ever at a loss for words, although sometimes they were the wrong words, and very often charmingly mispronounced. I had been prowling the blocks and blocks of bookstores in Tokyo's Kanda district, buying large numbers of dictionaries and Japanese readers. Some of the books promised speedy mastery of the language: I still have *Easy Japanese, Japanese in Three Weeks, Japanese in a Hurry,* and even *Japanese in Thirty Hours.* I found several Japanese-English primers, and bought them for the class. It was a delight to hear Richi-san read from them:

" 'Su-pring has-a come. U-arm u-inds bee-gin to bu-low. Gu-reen reaves come to the tu-rees.' Papa-san, this u-ord I don' know. Verree difficult!"

She could say "difficult" quite well, and she used the word often. I heard about an English class that would be starting at the Tokyo Y.W.C.A., and found that a course there cost only a couple of dollars a month, so I offered to pay Richi-san's tuition if she would enroll. She attended this class faithfully for several weeks, and certainly she learned some English there. But then:

"Papa-san, verree difficult! I cannot, that school. Bee-cause ozzer students just young girls, verree smart head—maybe college. I'm not smart head, and *not* college—just high school."

Perhaps, too, there was an atmosphere of Christianity in the Y.W.C.A., which, of course, would have been only proper. But Richi-san is a Nicheren Buddhist.

"Papa-san, when I was young girl, I was sinking about maybe bee-coming Kurisuchan. But maybe not good idea. I was sinking I cannot be anysing but just imitation Kurisuchan. So, don' changee. All right, Papa-san?"

I told her she had made a wise choice, because the world already had far too many imitation Christians, and then I advised her to drop out of the Y.W.C.A. school. The course was mainly designed to teach girls English so they could work for American or English business firms or for the American Security Forces. Richi-san did not intend to try to get a job with the American Security Forces. She and Yoshii-san had gone to Yokosuka, one day, to visit Goto-san's former painting instructor, who now ran an art shop there. Sailors and Marines whistled at them and made wolf calls as they walked from the railway station, and both girls were shocked and frightened. Richi-san told me that Yoshii-san walked faster, looked straight ahead, and kept saying in Japanese, "I am married u-oman! I am married u-oman!" Richi-san said she would never live or work near any of the American bases. . . .

Richi-san had been studying too much at night, and the rooms of the apato—like almost all Japanese rooms—were lighted only by single 50-watt bulbs. She had to get up very early to catch various buses if she made it on time to the Y.W.C.A. classes. After she dropped out of the course her health was better.

"Papa-san?"

"Yes, Richi-san?"

"Last night was verree good sleep—too muchee good sleep! Now I'm all time good helse. Never sickness."

"That's wonderful. Congratulations."

"What meaning 'congraturations,' Papa-san?"

"You didn't pronounce it right. 'Congratulations.'"

"I'm sorree, Papa-san. Congrat-*ul-ations*. What meaning?"

"I'll find it for you in the dictionary."

She looked and nodded, and said it was "verree in-ter-*est*-ing" and told me the Japanese word was maybe "shukuga." Then she said, "Yiss, I'm all time enjoyness good helse, Papa-san. But Next Door Wife-san *not* good helse—verree sorree to her. She's all time just a rittle—just a little stomachy. And coming her face many little, small pickles."

"You don't mean pickles, Richi-san. Pickles are tsukemono."

"Ah, so—not pickles?" She gave me a delightfully unabashed gamin smile. "Purples, Papa-san?"

"No. Purple is a color—murasaki."

"Ah, so-o? Maybe I'm meaning pinnacles?"

"No! Look it up in the dictionary!"

She did, and laughed for a moment, and then began all over again. "Coming her face, all time, many little pu-imples. Verree sorree to her."

None of the Many Cousins had much money to spend on any form of amusement, beyond an occasional cheap movie, and when first I went to Japan television had not yet arrived. As a result, I think they had a larger appreciation of something we have lost in America: the fun of family gatherings, the enjoyment of little games, the appreciation of conversation. After the English lessons, or after we had eaten sukiyaki, small talk and neighborhood gossip flowered. Over cups of Honorable Tea, Richi-san and her girl cousins chattered musically, and then—too polite to leave me long out of the conversation—Richi-san would translate. Before her English improved, this was sometimes verree difficult for both of us.

"Papa-san?"

"Yes, Richi-san?"

"We talking about Next Door Pretty Soon Wife-san. Five days bee-fore, she was going to countree—tu-rain going. She has two small babies. Three people going to countree. Understand, Papa-san?"

The lady who lived pretty soon from next door had gone to the country on the train, taking her two small children. I nodded.

"Yiss, Papa-san," and Richi-san's voice went up an octave in excitement. "Verree small baby—maybe five yu-ears old—going toilet. Don' stay train. Muzzer is verree u-orry [worried]! She's telephone many stations, cannot finding that small baby. Zo-o . . ."

I had not yet ridden many Japanese trains. I remembered early railroads in West Texas where you raised the lid of the accommodation and saw the ground flashing beneath, and they told an old story about the engineer who waited until you sat down and then ran over a thorny mesquite bush. I said, "Good Lord! You mean the baby fell through the toilet on the train?"

Richi-san had ridden many Japanese trains, and knew they were quite modern. She looked shocked.

"Of-a course not, Papa-san!" she said indignantly. "Don' fall toilet—cannot falling toilet! Fall out u-indow!"

"Fell out the window while the train was running?"

"Yiss."

"Why, the child could have been killed!"

"Yiss, I sink so. But not killed, Papa-san. Boy was finding small baby and taking to hospital. She's arm bu-roke and head cut— verree ba-ad cut. Sorree to that baby."

"Well, where is she now? How is she?"

"Now, Papa-san? Oh, today stay home. Come back her house day bee-fore yesterday. Last night I'm giving to her small present. Cake—two piece. She's speaking, 'Sank you verree muchee!'" Richi-san lifted the kettle and used the tongs to rearrange the glowing charcoal. "You don' cold, Papa-san?"

"No—I mean yes, I'm not cold, thank you. Are you cold?"

Richi-san beamed at the opportunity to use the answer she could give in almost perfect English:

"No, I am qu-wite comfortable, sank you."

THREE

TOKYO BETWEEN MEALS

I HAD BEEN IN JAPAN FOR A CONSIDERABLE TIME BEFORE RICHI-san's parents came from their "countree" to live in Tokyo, and brought with them a vast new store of folklore and custom and geographical knowledge of the land—all of which Richi-san translated for me. She called her father and mother O-jii-chan and O-baa-chan, or Honorable Little Grandfather and Honorable Little Grandmother. The other members of the Asano clan—and even casual acquaintances—called them by those titles, too. *Chan* is the affectionate diminutive of *san,* and is particularly applied to the very young and the very old; anyone who has become a grand-parent has attained a more respected estate than a mere father or mother, hence the title of greater honor. Incidentally, O-ji-san and O-ba-san mean Honorable Uncle and Honorable Aunt—it is the long "ii" and the long "aa" that make the difference.

O-jii-chan and O-baa-chan brought Richi-san's little daughter, Masako-chan, with them, and Richi-san was very happy. They found a larger apato in the Ogu-machi district of Tokyo, and from all over the city and its environs came the younger generations of the Asano family to do the elders honor, bring presents, report on the state of their affairs, and listen respectfully to O-jii-chan's comment or advice. This was a refreshing thing to see. In America, where people try to conceal their age, one may remark—with fond disrespect—that Grandpa, the poor old guy, has lost his marbles. This means that Grandpa has grown childish, and nobody pays any attention to him any more. You would not be likely to hear that in Japan, where age is clothed with such wisdom and dignity that a man will often pretend to be ten or fifteen years older than he actually is, so that he will be heard and honored in council. Japan is a wonderful place for babies and patriarchs.

Masako-chan, six and about to enter school, was a living Oriental doll. She had pigtails and a heart-shaped face, big, beautifully tilted eyes and a clear, golden skin, and she was very shy. Nobody had ever spanked her; indeed, no one ever raised his voice to her.

O-baa-chan, plump and serene and smiling, had graying hair and russet apple cheeks and always appeared to be wearing vast layers of kimono. She was incessantly busy at some household task, but she managed the apato so effortlessly that no one knew it was being managed at all.

O-jii-chan I had met before, on occasional trips he made to Tokyo, but now I had occasion to study him more closely. He was a short and sturdy man in his seventies, with a much younger face, and he wore glasses that gave him an owlish look and belied his frequent and hearty bursts of laughter. He enjoyed good food, but always ate everything that was put before him; he spent at least an hour every evening in the deep hot bath so dear to the Japanese, and in his eyes none of his grandchildren could do any wrong. Richi-san gave me a perfect thumbnail portrait of O-jii-chan:

"Papa-san, my fazzer is verree strangee man! Any kind fooding he can always eating, and he's enjoyness every people and everysing, verree muchee. He don' have a doesn't-like!"

A happy man—a fortunate man, indeed—who is without a single "doesn't-like."

Richi-san had told me, before her parents came, that O-jii-chan wanted to find some "ground" on which to build a house. Now that they had arrived, the search for a lot began in a way that was very vague and had the appearance of being hopeless, but at least it afforded me a chance of seeing more of Tokyo than I had seen. I had a jidosha, an automobile. It was a sports car, and could carry only three persons at the most, but I was frequently asked to make a Sunday drive to some remote part of the city, which would either turn out to be a district far too expensive or a slum much too wretched. There is too much of Tokyo, and it is growing at a fearful rate. Richi-san and the Many Cousins of the English class didn't know it, and neither did I until I found some statistics in books, but Tokyo (the name means Eastern Capital) was reportedly the second largest city in the world more than a hundred years ago. London was pushing a population of two million people in 1843, according to these records, and Paris had less than a million. Tokyo, a brash upstart of a town which then had only four hundred years of history, was between them. The cities of Kyoto, Osaka, Kobe, and Kamakura are much older than their big sister.

But Tokyo's comparatively brief history has been colorful, and has the advantage of having been fairly well recorded. It is difficult to separate history from O-jii-chan's folklore, and I have no desire to attempt doing so; it would take years to see all of the town and learn to know its many moods, or to sample the foods in thousands of little out-of-the-way eating places. Every day of the year there is an o-matsuri, or festival, going on somewhere, because Tokyo is not just one town, but many. When it was called Yedo (or Edo— either spelling is correct) more than sixteen hundred towns and villages stood among the marshes around the river mouth. "E" means inlet, and "do" was a portal, or doorway, a thousand years ago, when civilization was already highly developed at the ancient capital of Kyoto, and what is now Tokyo was only a cluster of fishermen's huts.

We drove around Tokyo to see prospective building lots or to visit Kyobashi Cousin, Shinogawa Cousin, Shinjuku Aunt and Unc', and various other members of the family; we stopped at shrines that looked ancient and interesting, and usually went by

the Tokyo Foreign Correspondents' Club in Shimbun Alley to
get Masako-chan some ice cream. I always had Richi-san attempt to
translate place names. She and all the Many Cousins, along with
the millions of their countrymen, are moved to poetry by the wind-
tuned lilt of April rain, by the mountain mists or the shimmering
magic of moonlight on the sea, by the pink-cloud beauty of flowering cherry trees, and by many a smaller loveliness. In a land which
can produce such names as Ko-ume-mura, or Little Plum Tree
Village, poetry is native. As a result, you find such places as the
Hill of the Crying Child, in Shinjuku. Richi-san located this for
me, and told me a story which does not belong to Japan alone—it
is found around the world, and used to crop up about once a year,
in my newspaper days, under datelines from Austria to India or
Australia. It deals with the poor farmer who is in desperate need
of money with which to entertain his son, coming home after long
years for a visit. The farmer kills a wayfarer and takes his purse.
The traveler, of course, is the son, bringing home a gift of money
to his parents. . . .

"Verree sad story, Papa-san," Richi-san said, and then gave a
charming shrug. "But can't be helped, that kind sing." And I never
did really learn how a crying child fit into the picture.

She learned, however, that I was interested in such place names,
and went out of her way to find them. They run through the
geography of Japan with a strong and lilting lure: every place has
its ancient legend and its special imagery. In the rugged Chichibu
range northwest of Tokyo, there is a mountain over which the wild
geese fly in their seasonal migrations, and from the valley below it
looks as if they are brushing the top. Therefore—and there are two
other mountains with the same name—the peak is called Gan-ga-
hara-zuri-yama, or Goose Scratching Belly Mountain. Who would
not travel all the way to the northern island of Hokkaido to see
Mount Hakodate, since it also is known as Gagyusan, or Recum-
bent Cow Mountain? And what about a bridge down in Iwakuni,
known as Kintai-bashi, or the Bridge of the Brocaded Sash?

One doesn't have to go that far. In Shinjuku, there is a span

Richi-san calls the Goo'-bye Bridge, although it has had many names. It seems there was a rich miser who had various servants dig holes in the ground where he buried his treasure. He was a suspicious and ungrateful sort, and always killed the diggers as they were returning over the bridge, so no one but himself would know where the money was hidden. It was goo'-bye to these simple and faithful retainers, but the miser met his come-uppance. (He had a ba-ad heart, Richi-san said.) His daughter came to a marriageable age and a match was made, but on her wedding night she was transformed into a hebi-san—a Mister Snake—and committed suicide by wriggling spectacularly off the bridge. Her father repented, and gave all his possessions to the Kumano Shrine. After that, the bridge became known as Namida-bashi, or Bridge of Tears.

But, Richi-san told me in a little restaurant where we ate o-sushi, or raw fish on pickled rice dumplings, that was five or six hundred years ago, and the name did not stick. During the seventeenth century, the bridge was officially named Yodo-bashi, and it is called that today.

"But, Papa-san, if girl just married crossing that bridge on u-edding day, she will never being happy! And sometimes people still looking [digging] for Kujuro-san's money, this place. Was ba-ad man!"

THE STORIES SHE TOLD WERE SOMETIMES HERS; SOMETIMES THEY had been related by O-jii-chan, or by Shinjuku Aunt and Unc'. I heard them in small restaurants where we tried kimchi, the peppery Korean dish, or had sashimi, which is raw fish, or ate the excellent Chinese food which can be found all over Tokyo. In fact, Tokyo is a gourmet's paradise. American food is available there, and so are French, German, Italian, Mexican, Russian, Armenian, East Indian, and Scandinavian dishes. Genghis Khan fare is broiled at your table, and there is a place seating only twelve people, in a suballey off an alley, not far from the Ginza, that serves skewered chicken livers, wild duck, pheasant, quail, and even sparrows, after suimono, a clear soup which is a dream of delicate flavor.

In the home of Shinjuku Aunt and Unc', I was introduced to unagikabayaki, or broiled eel. This was during the midsummer season, on the Day of the Cow, when everybody in Japan eats broiled eel. The eel is split open and skinned and boned, then cut into pieces impaled on several sharp bamboo skewers; it is broiled over charcoal, then steamed and dipped into specially prepared shoyu sauce and broiled again. I drool, remembering its flavor.

"Must eating unagi on Cow Day, Papa-san," Richi-san informed me earnestly. "Bee-cause, if unagi eating that day, you will not having sickness all year. Verree good for the body!"

I liked to eat my way through Tokyo, taking time out to see an ancient shrine, or go to a theater as modern as any in the world, or a huge department store with air conditioning and escalators. There are many who insist that Tokyo is not Japan, but a bastard conglomeration of East and West; they say one must see the old capital of Kyoto to appreciate thousands of years of representative Japanese arts and culture. Kyoto is beautiful, but I believe Tokyo is fully representative of Japan and of the energetic and adaptable spirit of its people. It was here that the marshes of the Musashino Plain were drained, and a city more fabulous than Xanadu was decreed, and came in to being. It is in Tokyo that one sees at its best the Japanese art of adaptation. This is quite different, actually, from imitation.

We called on Kyobashi Cousin, who lives only a little way from the noisy and crowded Ginza and not far from Nihonbashi. The latter is the ancient bridge—rebuilt many times—from which all distances in Japan are measured.

"That name, Papa-san, was bee-cause on this bridge can seeing sun coming up and sun going down, goo'-bye."

It also is where the Ginza really begins. People ginbura (stroll on the Ginza) on soft evenings. Richi-san liked to window-shop as much as does any American woman.

"Papa-san, you 'ant ginbura? I like verree muchee. Just look, don' buy—"

Walking down the showcased Ginza, it is not easy to remember that Tokyo was once the garrison town of Yedo, where swaggering, two-sworded samurai outnumbered the civilian residents. The shadowy emperors lived in Kyoto in those days; the real ruler was the shogun, who maintained a splendid palace in Yedo and required all the feudal lords (daimyo, or honored names) to spend a part of each year there—the better to be taxed. The daimyo brought their private armies of samurai. This was an Occupation long before MacArthur's and one less just or kind. Samurai ranked first in society under the nobility; farmers were second, and honest artisans, such as carpenters and barbers, were third. A tradesman—anybody who handled money—was at the very bottom of the scale.

"That time, Papa-san, if somebody keeping store, was called chonin. Oh, verree ba-ad, being chonin! Cannot keeping sword, and don' have last name—just first name having—and samurai can killing, any time!"

It seems that a large number of the chonin were expended, in those days, to blood the swords of the samurai. But the Japanese are a very patient race. The merchants survived, multiplied, and got rich on the Yedo population and land boom. A new order was born, and they were able to hold their own against the military. They produced a style of art, literature, and drama peculiar to their town; it was based on riches and pleasure, and now it is traditional. Edokko, as the people of Tokyo are still called, became noted for being spendthrift and loving luxury. This survives today. An Osaka man will ask, "How is business?" and a Tokyo resident will want to know if you are having a good time.

Under the guidance of Richi-san and others of the Asano family I toured Tokyo and its food. It is perhaps hardest of all to find real Japanese food, except for the soba (noodle) wagons on the street corner—and these, actually, offer Chinese noodles. There is a rather expensive place called Furusato, in Shibuya Ward, that occupies a house moved from Gifu Prefecture and reported to be eight hundred years old, and the food there is authentically Japanese. Fireplaces are sunk in the floor; waitresses in colorful costume do folk dances from Akita-ken, or Akita Prefecture. Richi-san was most impressed by these dances, and told me the Japanese have a saying, or kotowaza (proverb):

"Japanese people speaking, Papa-san, Akita-ken having Number One sake, and Number One dogs, and Number One pretty girls in Japan."

"Did you come from Akita-ken?" I teased.

Richi-san blushed. "Oh, no—never! My family coming Miyagi-ken. You knows Miyagi-ken—maybe same like next door Akita-ken."

Furusato specializes in chawan-mushi, a custard of meat, fish, chicken, eggs and vegetables. It serves eel on tofu, or bean curd, and all are delicious. Between the lowly noodle wagons and the places like Furusato is a wide range of o-sushi bars and sukiyaki and tempura restaurants (tempura is sea food fried in deep fat). The latter two can be found in America; the other dishes, in poor imitation, are available only in San Francisco and New York. I have met many Americans who were aghast at the idea of eating raw fish.

"Do you like oysters or clams on the half shell?"

"Oh, of course! But raw fish—never!"

They eat raw fish in Italy, in the Caribbean, in Hawaii, and probably in many other places outside Japan. I submit that nothing is more raw than an oyster, complete with viscera. Sashimi, on the other hand, consists principally of lean—almost dry—slices of tuna or other varieties of boneless fish. Anyone who tries it comes back for more.

Of course, there are even more unusual and exotic foods to be found in Tokyo, along with a few drinks that go beyond sake and biru (beer). I did not try them. For the most part, I was eating with members of the Asano family, and they had never tried grass-hoppers, or chocolate-dipped bees and ants, or even the blowfish, which must be prepared in a very careful way lest it kill everybody who eats it. Nobody ever offered me broiled stripe snake, or broiled viper either; I don't think these are really typical of the food of the country. But one day after O-jii-chan and O-baa-chan had come to Tokyo, Richi-san did stop on the street to buy a bottle of brown powder from a peddler.

This was powdered snake. O-baa-chan believed, implicitly, that a little powdered snake, taken after meals, was an excellent spring tonic.

After that, Richi-san showed me a small bar.

"There place, Papa-san, selling su-nake wine. Verree expensive, su-nake wine. Putting su-nake in bottle of verree strong sake, and keeping maybe three years. You 'ant drinking that kind, Papa-san?"

"No, thank you," I said. "Make mine biru."

I have not known any Japanese who drinks wine poured off a pickled snake, although it is reported that it is sold by at least forty bars in Tokyo. It seems to me this beverage is an open invitation to delirium tremens. I know of no other drink that comes equipped with built-in snakes.

FOUR

A JAGUAR IN JAPAN

ONE WAY TO SEE THE LOVELY COUNTRYSIDE AROUND TOKYO IS TO travel with the Sports Car Club of Japan, which is a very cosmopolitan group. Its membership used to be made of about fifty per cent Japanese, forty per cent American, and ten per cent British and other nationalities, including Chinese. It was hand-in-glove with the Japanese Automobile Association, the equivalent of our A.A.A., and buddy-buddy with the Japanese police, and this opened a lot of roads. Its emblem showed a knock-off wire wheel surmounted by a torii (gate), and bore the club's name in katakana, while the membership card said, with a fine international flair, "Pour le grand sport." When I went on rallies with the Sports Car Club, I usually took Richi-san along as my gaido.

She could read the confusing road signs, navigate us through the small villages, and tell me folk stories about places she had never seen before but had read about. But she was never half so enchanted with the Jaguar roadster as her cousin Goto-san had always been. Richi-san preferred what she called "sid-downs," because sedans protected her from the weather. She could never understand why I didn't put up the top.

41

"Papa-san, today don' put on cover?"

"Oh, not today! It's so sunny and nice. Why, are you cold?"

"No, not, Papa-san. But my hair will being verree broke and my face will too muchee brown!"

Telling her that wind-blown bobs and sun tans were very fashionable in the States did not console her, although she admired America and American women. She was horrified at the thought of not being well groomed. There were occasions when I learned on Saturday evening that the Sports Car Club had scheduled a "mystery" rally for Sunday morning. Cars were to assemble at ten o'clock in Meiji Park, where drivers would be given limited mimeographed instructions. The final destination would be Nikko or Hakone, perhaps, and the general route was revealed. But instruments were blacked out, and widely varying rates of speed would have to be estimated between eight or ten check points, locations not given, along the way. Competitors could lose points equally by being too fast or too slow, because a test car had previously made the run and logged mileage and elapsed time.

I went to the Ogu-machi apato at nine on Sunday morning. "Sports Car rally!" I told Richi-san. "Hurry, if you want to go, because we must be at Meiji Park before ten."

"Oh, yiss, Papa-san! But first I must bath taking. Just a moment."

Nobody yet has taken an ofuro in a hurry. The ofuro was not meant to be hurried; it is a ritual, long and leisurely, as O-jii-chan so well knows. The public bath house was a block away.

"But, Richi-san, we will have very dusty roads, and it will do no good to take a bath. You can have one this evening—you'll need it then. Didn't you have a bath last evening?"

"Oh, yiss, of course. But I cannot anywhere going wizzout bath —*must* bath, Papa-san. Japanese custom."

The time was growing late. The cars would already be gathering at Meiji Park, where the Imperial Army used to hold its parades; the other drivers would be studying the instructions and making last-minute carburetor adjustments and (what had I just told Richi-san about the roads?) wiping off their machines. And here was

Richi-san going off down the narrow alleyway with her wooden geta clicking musically, carrying her little brass wash basin with its soap and toothbrush and towel and comb, to come back half an hour later scrubbed and glowing. Then:

"What put on, Papa-san? Panties put on?"

I smiled. "I think perhaps you mean slacks. I think I told you before—ladies *always* wear panties. Sometimes, for sports events, they wear slacks. In the States some women should never, never wear slacks, on pain of death or divorce. But most Japanese girls can wear slacks."

By this time Richi-san was giggling, but she waited until I had finished the language lesson.

"I'm sorree, Papa-san—I'm forget! I'm meaning sracks—slacks— not panties. Just a moment, Papa-san."

She vanished inside the apato, to spend another fifteen or twenty minutes at her dressing table, which was the small Japanese variety before which a woman has to kneel. If we made Meiji Park in time, it was only with a minute to spare, and because I took a chance of being tagged for speeding.

FOR ONE EVENT, A HUNDRED-MILE RUN TO NIKKO AND BEAUTIFUL Lake Chuzenji in the mountains beyond, we were late at the starting point, and I mourned the race as already lost. Richi-san calmly advised me, "Papa-san don' u-orry about it," and we headed out on the road—the last car. I growled and complained; we passed the first check point, and I was sure we were many minutes behind. We rolled through farming country, where the unpaved roads were thick with summer dust and it was sometimes impossible to pass trucks. When we came finally to long, open stretches, Richi-san said, "Papa-san, I must ladies' room."

"Ladies' room!" I exclaimed. "Where? I haven't seen a gas station in ten miles. There are no ladies' rooms!"

"Papa-san, please stopping that place—I will asking."

She indicated a farmhouse at the side of the road. We were

losing points. Besides, one just doesn't go into a private residence and ask such favors.

"Konnichi-wa!" Richi-san greeted a man working in a field by the house. "Gofujo, arimasuka?"

The man made a low bow. "Arimasu, dozo!" ("There is—please!") And he courteously showed her the way.

I sat beating the steering wheel, certain that we were losing the race ignominiously, and borrowed a phrase from Richi-san's English when I saw how politely she was welcomed. "Never happen in States!" I told myself. She returned, and we fled on along the dusty road, and after more check points came to one of the most beautiful highways anywhere. It was lined by the giant cryptomeria trees which I have seen only in Japan; they surpass the lovely poplars of Lombardy. Richi-san told me their story. More than two centuries ago, when the famous Toshogu shrines were being built at Nikko, the Japanese nobles set up elaborate and expensive stone and metal lanterns there, to honor the spirit of Iyeyasu Tokugawa, who had founded the long-ruling Tokugawa Shogunate. Masatsuna Matsudaira, one of the feudal lords, had fallen upon poverty. He could not afford to donate lanterns. Instead, he planted forty thousand cryptomeria saplings to border twenty-five miles of the avenues leading to the shrines. More than eighteen thousand of the trees stand today, a rich memorial indeed.

We came into the town of Nikko, which is in one of the seventeen national parks of Japan. Most tourists go there. The Japanese, with their love for punning and word play, have a saying: "Do not speak kekkô until you've seen Nikko!" (Kekkô means "magnificent.")

"Oh, Papa-san—there place Shihonryuji Temple, verree famous place! And Sambutsu-do—we must looking!"

"We can't—we're out for points!" I said, looking at the masked speedometer instead of at the scenery. "We're behind schedule, and there must be fifteen miles or more to go."

"Ah, so, Papa-san." A moment of silence. "Papa-san, please stopping medicine shop. I must buying hair lotion."

A medicine shop is a drugstore, and hair lotion is shampoo. I cannot read Japanese signs; I can tell a medicine shop only by the goods displayed in its showcases. I kept driving.

"Why?" I asked irritably. "We're far behind."

"Oh, but I must hair lotion. Bee-cause too muchee dusting."

"But that's crazy, Richi-san! It'll be just as dusty in the next fifteen miles, up the mountains."

"Please, Papa-san! Just a moment!"

Doomed from the start, I thought. Lost from the beginning. It was no use; it didn't matter any more. I pulled over to the curb, and Richi-san went into the medicine shop. They didn't happen to sell the kind of shampoo she wanted, and we had to move on up the street a couple of blocks. She found it there, and was gone fifteen minutes—she was in the back room of the medicine shop, where they obligingly let her shampoo her hair.

Then she emerged, fresh and glowing again, and with bad grace I put the Jaguar in gear and drove on up the dusty mountain road to the big hotel at Lake Chuzenji, and an accounting.

I knew everything was lost. But I heard the rally steward calling my name, and I walked up to the speaker's table to receive a handsome silver cup.

We had won second place. There was exactly one minute's difference between our time and that of the Number One car.

"Tondemonai!" I told Richi-san as I came back to our table and sat down. "Never happen. I don't understand."

She only smiled. Her hair was already bu-roke and dusty after the shampooing fifteen miles back.

"Of-a course, Papa-san," she said. "I'm before telling you, don' u-orry about it. And, bee-sides, I'm praying to Buddha, this Su-ports Car Crub race."

GOTO-SAN AND SOME OF THE OTHER MANY COUSINS WOULD HAVE given their right arms to go with me on a Sports Car Club rally, but their English was not enough to be of any real help. Richi-san loved Su-ports Car Crub meetings, but I don't think she really

ever understood what we were trying to do. It was childish play to
her, and she was tolerant about it, but not about the dust and wind.
And there were other hazards. Japanese villagers have a commendable habit of wetting down the street in front of their houses or shops
in the dry season; they do this with buckets of water, and a car as
low as the Jaguar is extremely vulnerable. On one rally, a shop-
keeper who was energetically settling the dust in front of his
establishment threw a bucket of water against the side of the car
and splashed me a little. No damage was done, but Richi-san was
furious for hours. "Watsamatta that man, Papa-san?" she asked
darkly. "Don' look, just nageru [throw]! *Ba-ad* heart, I sink so.
Maybe baka [idiot]! I sink so."

She was always tired before a Sports Car Club rally was finished,
and glad to get home; she frequently did something very few people
can do—she fell asleep in an open sports car, with the sun on her
face and the wind tugging at her hair, and I had to wake her and
tell her she was home. Then she would say, "Sank you verree
muchee, Papa-san—now I must bath taking. Today, muchee enjoyness."

There was an event which called for the gaido to stand in the
seat and lance toy balloons with a six-foot bamboo pole that was
tipped with a needle. The balloons were tied on the ground along
a quarter mile stretch of country road, with a wire fence on one
side and a ditch on the other. It was anything but a speed event,
since the ditch had to be crossed again and again to get to the
balloons on that side. Richi-san thought this was childish sport,
indeed, and hardly worthy of her age, much less mine. But when
our turn came to go and the starting flag was dropped, she entered
into the spirit of the occasion and broke the balloons with a will.
We negotiated the course nine seconds faster than any other of the
more than twenty cars, and she was acclaimed by one of my friends
as the Number One Balloon Buster of Japan.

"Sank you verree muchee," she said, laughing, and then turned
to me. "Papa-san, what means 'buster'?"

"Breaker," I said. "You broke the balloons faster than anybody else. So you keep the silver cup."

"Oh, sank you—it will verree good memory for today!"

But we were not always so lucky, nor was Richi-san always so helpful as a copilot. We sat in the car one Sunday morning in Yokohama, second in line for a hare and hounds event. The cars were leaving one minute apart; the "hare" a red MG with "HARE" painted boldly across its spare wheel cover, had just roared away. The first "hound" moved up and was off, and we were waiting the starter's flag.

"Papa-san?"

"Yes, Richi-san?"

"What means 'harreh,' English speaking?"

" 'Harreh'? Oh—you mean hare. It means rabbit—usagi. That red MG was the rabbit, and we are the dogs—inu. Understand?"

"I don' sink so, Papa-san—I don' understand. Japanese speaking, 'harreh' means just a little stomachy and fine wezzer. I don' understand English meaning."

The flag dropped, and we roared away into the Yokohama traffic. A score of takushi-cabs and trucks had already insinuated themselves between us and the first car; the hare was well down the street by now. We were to try to overtake him, and, failing that, to rendezvous at Lake Hakone at lunchtime. But it is disconcerting to start out on any kind of enterprise with such incongruities as "a little stomachy" and "fine wezzer" left hanging in the air. At a traffic light, I hurriedly scanned the dictionary. Sure enough, the Japanese word *hare* means a stomach tumor, and another word spelled the same way in romaji (but having a different kanji character) means clear weather.

"I see," I told Richi-san as we drove on. "But that's why Japanese is so difficult—two words pronounced the same, but with different meaning."

"English easy, Papa-san?"

"Of course it is. H-a-r-e—we don't pronounce it 'harreh,' like you do. We call it hare. Like the hair on your head, only it is spelled different."

"I understand, Papa-san. But I sink English verree difficult."

We drove on a few miles, leaving Yokohama behind, and rolling down the ancient Tokkaido Highway—the name means East Sea Road—which is Japan's Route 1. Neither of us had been that way before. We saw none of the other sports cars, and I began to wonder if we were still on the road to Lake Hakone.

"Do you think this is right, Richi-san?"

"Right?" She held up her right hand. "Migi?"

"No—this is a different kind of right. You see, we have two or three—er—several English words pronounced the same. We have r-i-g-h-t, meaning migi, and w-r-i-t-e, meaning to write a letter, and r-i-t-e, meaning—"

"Oh, Papa-san, I'm forget. Yesterday coming to my room a letter. Shinjuku aunt and unc' speaking, 'Harro, Papa-san.' They said."

"Well, thank you. Tell your Shinjuku aunt and uncle hello for me. But, as I started to say, do you think this is the right road— the true road—to Hakone?"

"Papa-san stop. I will risten—listen."

"You'll what?"

"I will listen."

Somewhat mystified, I pulled to the curb and stopped. Her meaning became clear: she would ask a question and listen for the answer. She hailed a Japanese woman who wore kimono and had a baby strapped on her back. They bowed. They exchanged pleasantries and greetings, salutations and amenities. Each chattered at length, while the other nodded and said, "Ah, so?" or "Ha-ha," or, "So desu ne?" or just plain "Ne?" which means "You see?" or "Isn't it so?" and is almost entirely a feminine word—nobody could ever speak it the way a Japanese woman does.

Such a conversation passes the time. This was turning out as the run to Nikko had threatened to do: the other cars were somewhere down the road, probably on the *right* road, perhaps overtaking the hare and making points. I filled and lighted my pipe while Richi-san and the woman talked; I sweated around the collar, and thumbed through my Japanese dictionary, and wondered how we could have gotten so far off the route to require such lengthy directions. The dictionary showed many words to support my contention that spoken Japanese is more complicated than English. Here was an example: it listed nineteen words, all spelled koko (most of them with long "o" sounds) which meant a wide variety of things, from "here" to "pickles," "filial piety," and "sailing." And, to my untutored eye, the kanji characters for all these appeared to be very much alike.

Finally, Richi-san and the woman each bowed three times. The baby, asleep on the woman's back, bowed too, its neck in danger of snapping. They both murmured "Domo arigato!" in thanks, and then, "Sumimasen," which is softly slurred to sound like "Sooey-mah-sen" and means "I'm sorry to have troubled you." Then they said, "Sayonara!"

I put the car into gear. Richi-san turned to me, her small face glowing with good will.

"Verree kindness, Papa-san! Good heart, don' you?"

"Yes, she is a very kind woman. She has a good heart."

"Yiss, I sink so."

"But what about the road? What about the road to Hakone?"

"Oh, Papa-san, Hakone road she don' know."

WE FOUND A ROAD SIGN, AND WE FOUND BEAUTIFUL LAKE HAKONE in its Alps-like setting, and the other sports cars. But we won no trophy that day. And returning through downtown Tokyo in the early evening, there was another language hassle. Richi-san pointed to the Northwest Airlines sign on the Nikkatsu Hotel.

"What speaking that sign, Papa-san?" she asked while we were waiting for a traffic light.

"Northwest Airlines," I said. "It's the name of an airplane company. It means between north and west—kita and nishi."

"Verree strangee," said Richi-san. "I'm always before sinking that sign means 'don' u-orry about it!'"

I puzzled over this for quite a while. "Does Northwest sound like something that means don't worry about it?"

"Yiss, of course, Papa-san."

Safety in flight? She wouldn't know that. An idea occurred to me, but it didn't seem logical. Richi-san had never been exposed to GI slang.

"Was it 'no sweat,' maybe?"

"Oh, yiss—that word, Papa-san. No sweat."

"But where did you learn that word?"

"Oh, I sink my friend, Toshiko-san. I don' telling you about Toshiko-san. Old friend. She's married nisei boy—American sergeant."

That explained everything. To me, the Northwest Airlines will always be the No-Sweat Airlines, and when flying with them don' u-orry about it.

FIVE

A PIKUNIKKU

KAMI-WARI, WHICH MEANS GOD CUTTING OPEN, IS A GREAT PINE-clad rock standing in the mouth of Togura Bay, on the northeast coast of the main Japanese island of Honshu. The place is off the track even for Japanese vacationists, and probably no more than a score of American tourists have ever looked upon its rugged beauty or visited Shizukawa, the remote fishing village that is the nearest town. Neither place is listed in the guidebooks. But Richi-san and all the basic family of the Asanos originally came from Shizukawa—it is their countree—and, like other natives of the picturesque place, they are very proud of Kami-wari as a scenic reminder of divine wrath. Even before I went there from Tokyo with the Asanos, I had heard the story from them several times.

The story goes like this: In the ancient chronicles it was written that on a night when the sea came shouting across the rocks, and lanterns would not stay alight, a whale was stranded on the rocky beach between two rival communities—Togura-mura and the Thirteen Villages, the latter a series of small hamlets strung along a narrow neck of land, and all getting their luck upon the sea.

Each community claimed the whale as its rightful bounty. A bitter quarrel raged all the next day, and that night an awesome thing happened. The rocky neck of land split open, and the sea rushed in, dividing the two communities forever. "Kami-wari!" the frightened people cried. "God cutting open!" Thus the place was named. But there are few scholars able to read the ancient scrolls—if, indeed, the scrolls still exist—and it is best to hear the story as I did, from the lips of Richi-san, whose English has always been especially charming to me since I cast her in the role of Galatea.

"Zo-o it was, Papa-san," Richi-san said, retelling the story on the day I went for a picnic with her and her family and saw Kami-wari. She and I were watching the clear Pacific run green and white between the towering rock walls of the cleft. "There was too muchee troubling, and God was verree angree. That night, God cutting open rocks, and ocean bumping bee-tween, and people verree su'pris*ed* and scared. That story maybe two sousand years old. I lovely that story. Understand, Papa-san?"

"I understand," I said, and pointed to the inhospitable chunk of granite that had been riven from the mainland. "But don't you think that place was very small to hold a village?"

"Oh, yiss, of course, Papa-san," she agreed. "But it was a verree small whale."

THE TRIP TO SHIZUKAWA HAD BEEN LONG IN THE MAKING BEFORE we actually went. It was summer in Tokyo, and before O-jii-chan and O-baa-chan built their new house they wanted to make a pilgrimage to the place of their ancestors during O-Bon, the Buddhist Festival of the Dead. In some parts of Japan, O-Bon is observed in July; in Shizukawa, by the ancient lunar calendar and by local custom, it falls in August. The Asanos said they would like to show me their countree when they gathered at the family shrine in Shizukawa to honor the spirits of their ancestors.

"What kind of country is it?" I asked.

"Oh, verree pretty place, Papa-san! Su-mall mounts and beeg ocean. Can fishing and su-wimming, and-a noise don' have."

Tokyo has had the reputation of being the noisiest city in the world. I told Richi-san it was a deal.

"What means 'deal,' Papa-san?"

"I mean I accept your invitation with pleasure. Thank you very much."

"Sank *you* verree muchee, Papa-san," she said.

O-Bon is comparable to our All Souls' Day, and calls for a three-day reunion of the Japanese family to worship before the mortuary tablets of its ancestors and to make a report on family affairs to the ancestral spirits. All over Japan, white lanterns shed their glow on family altars. Sutras are chanted slowly and sonorously, with full intonations of "Na-mu-myo ho ren-ge-kyo!" ("Glory to the Supreme Law of the Lotus!") Prayer beads click briskly, incense burns, and choice food offerings are made. There is no sadness in any of this; the spirits are treated as living persons. The streets are bright with bonfires to light the way of the spirits to their former homes, and the night is lively with fireworks and drumbeat, with the soft shine of serpentine lantern parades, and with dancing.

Some of the Asano family—I will never know exactly how many—are still in residence in Shizukawa, but enough others made the pilgrimage there from Tokyo to put a strain on the already crowded coaches of the Jôban railroad line. Half the population of Japan seemed to be making similar pilgrimages, and it was just as well that the Tokyo Asano clan didn't go en masse, but traveled by echelons. When we were finally gathered in Shizukawa, our party included O-jii-chan and O-baa-chan as living heads of the family; four O-ji-san, or uncles; several O-ba-san, or aunts (these, belonging to both sides of the family, came and went in profusion); two Ne-san, or older sisters; two brothers and their wives; seven grandchildren, a number of cousins; Richi-san; Masako-chan, and me. Fortunately, the ancestral house is quite large.

All this was fitting, since O-Bon offers the perfect excuse for a reunion of the living with the living, as well as with the dead. But, to begin with, it posed certain logistical problems, because no Japanese ever goes anywhere without taking along at least one puresento (present) for everybody else who will be there, and, therefore, the luggage that each echelon carried with it from Tokyo was mountainous.

It seemed that there were also more special problems affecting this particular trip. When it became known that I had accepted Richi-san's invitation, O-jii-chan promptly left for Shizukawa more than a week in advance of my prospective arrival, to arrange for a hotel room for me and make other preparations to do me honor. A few days later, a letter came from the country for Honorable Little Grandmother. Richi-san told me that her elder brother's wife, who lived in Shizukawa, was worried about "special fooding" for me.

"Papa-san, 'hat kind special fooding you 'ant?" Richi-san asked.

"None," I assured her hastily. "No special food at all. I will stay at the hotel."

"Oh, yiss, I sink so. But *not* good fooding at that hotel. You must eating at our house, and my countree is very poor countree. Bifuteki [beefsteak] don' have."

"It doesn't matter," I said. "I can get along without beefsteak for a few days."

Richi-san said she didn't sink so, *not* getting along without beef-steak for a few days, bee-cause I had a beeg body and must every day eating meat. She said that in her countree there was only fish and chicken, and "sometimes peeg." I reminded her that the many members of the family I had met, most of whom grew up in Shizu-kawa, showed no signs of malnutrition. I pointed out that O-jii-chan had attained a ripe old age, and that Honorable Little Grandmother looked the way little grandmothers all over the world ought to look —apple cheeked and plump—and still had her own teeth. I told Richi-san not to worry about it.

"Papa-san don' u-orry about it!" she retorted, and wrote a letter to the country about "special fooding" for me. I don't know what it said.

Then Richi-san and Honorable Little Grandmother, left in charge of the last Tokyo echelon, concluded that I ought not to make the journey alone. I couldn't get leave until the day before

O-Bon began, and they felt that I couldn't speak enough Japanese to travel by myself, so they decided that they would delay their own departure by almost a week to escort me. Masako-chan, who had been attending school in Tokyo, would go with us.

"No, no!" I protested. "Masako-chan has only a short school vacation. You go on and enjoy the country."

"Don' u-orry about it," Richi-san said.

That is how I found myself on the crowded express from Ueno Station with three females—O-baa-chan, Richi-san, and Masako-chan—all four of us us a little confused as to who was escorting whom. We were bound for Sendai, where we would transfer from the train to a bus for Shizukawa. The luggage racks and the space between the seats were piled high with my bags, typewriter, and camera equipment, their suitcases, and the many beautifully wrapped puresentos.

The station purattohomu (platform) was jammed with holidaying humanity, and once aboard the train we were lucky to find seats. "Papa-san, we must being careful," Richi-san confided with a frown. "O-baa-chan and Masako-chan are verree countree girls—never before anywhere going. Maybe happen troubling, I sink so."

I laughed, and said I was sure no trouble would happen.

TRAVEL IN A JAPANESE TRAIN COMBINES THE OLD NOSTALGIC CHARM of rail-click and drawn-out whistle with something of military pomp and circumstance. Stationmasters and purattohomu officials snap to salute as the train pulls out, the train crew responds, and an air of tremendous importance surrounds the whole undertaking. Frequently there are large parties on the purattohomu to bid sayonara to a departing notable or company executive. When the train pulls out, they bow in succession as the honored traveler glides past them. Soon the train is in the suburbs, where every crossing has its throng of pedestrians and cyclists waiting behind a single slender bamboo barrier. Then the little wooden houses become scattered, the evergreen countryside opens wide, and everywhere are shining waterways.

Watanabe-san, the average Japanese, knows how to ride trains in hot weather. He comes aboard wearing long cotton drawers, like pajama lowers, under his business suit; he brings his fan and a pair of soft slippers. As soon as he finds a seat, he removes his hot business suit and his necktie, folding them neatly, and gets out of his shoes. Then he buys beer or pots of honorable tea from the purattohomu vendors, and settles back to fan himself, doze, or read his morning newspaper.

We had scarcely left Tokyo when O-baa-chan, the countree girl, sat on the seat cushion with her feet tucked behind her in Japanese fashion, leaned against the back rest, and promptly fell asleep. The Japanese ability to sleep anywhere and at any time is matched only by another national elasticity, the ability to eat food or drink tea whenever either is offered. There were people sitting on their luggage in the aisles of the coaches—all drinking tea and eating bento, the Japanese version of a box lunch—and littering the aisles with tangerine peelings. The porter swept often, but it was not enough. The trip from Tokyo to Sendai took six and a half hours, and the litter grew, but there was no troubling beyond having to raise the window at every stop for somebody who wanted to buy bento or ice cream. In fact, everything went smoothly until we reached Sendai, the largest and most important city in northeastern Japan. But then, into that city of some four hundred thousand, O-baa-chan, a little old lady wearing a blue polka-dot dress and shod in Japanese zori (flat-soled sandals), vanished shortly after we got off the train.

Honorable Little Grandmother's disappearance came about simply enough, through a takushi-cab mixup and the fact that she did something few Japanese women of her generation have ever done—she took the initiative. Because of our luggage, we found it necessary to hire two of the small, pomade-scented cabs to transport us from the Sendai railway station to the Basu Senta (the Bus Center) from which we were to continue our journey to Shizukawa. Our bags completely filled the rear seat of the first cab, and Honorable Little Grandmother, unbidden, plopped herself in the front seat beside the driver, determined to keep an eye on my typewriter, which she regards with respect. At that moment, a station official appeared, bowing and sucking in his breath politely, to inform Richi-san that certain minor irregularities had been found in our train tickets. She would have to visit the Fare Adjustment Office. When she went off to do this, our Number One cab roared into traffic almost as dense as that of downtown Tokyo, carrying Honorable Little Grandmother into the unknown.

Masako-chan and I waited. We could see Richi-san through the windows of the Fare Adjustment Office, and it became apparent that even a minor irregularity could not be adjusted without the formalities. Richi-san bowed. The officials bowed. They exchanged amenities and spoke of the weather. It was explained to Richi-san that our tickets should have been used on the previous day; however, the Fare Adjustment Office would make a telephone call to Tokyo to confirm their validity. Then Richi-san bowed and thanked the station officials. They bowed and said, "It is this side which owes." She came back to the curb, and I explained why Honorable Little Grandmother was missing.

I suggested that we follow her as fast as possible, and we drove at once to the Bus Center, where, Richi-san said, all the people boarded all the buses for Shizukawa. When we got there, a long queue was waiting for the Shizukawa bus, but there was no sign of Honorable Little Grandmother or our luggage—not in the station, or in the bus, or among the people waiting in the queue. Then someone told Richi-san that there were now several other Basu Sentas in Sendai, and that Shizukawa buses left from some of them too. I joined the end of the queue for the next Shizukawa bus, to hold our place, while Richi-san and Masako-chan took a takushi-cab to search for O-baa-chan at the other stations.

Very shortly, they were back. No O-baa-chan anywhere. This time, I put them in the queue, and took a takushi-cab and toured the other stations myself. That search was fruitless too. I began trying to remember what O-baa-chan's takushi driver looked like. He had a sinister appearance, perhaps; he might have seen the type-

writer and the camera among the luggage piled in his back seat; he
could have driven O-baa-chan to some remote place, pushed her
out of the cab, and made off with the loot. With my imagination
working overtime I went back to the first Basu Senta to find that
Richi-san's previous calm was shaken.

"Papa-san," she said in a high treble, "I'm before telling you!
O-baa-chan is verree countree girl. She doesn' have good head. Too
muchee troubling!" She made a forceful gesture of boxing Honorable Little Grandmother's ears. "I'm verree angree to her!"

Richi-san's voice bordered on hisuteri (hysteria). I said, "I'm not
angry—I'm worried. We'd better tell the police."

"Don' need police! Not their busy-ness. Papa-san don' be children!" (She pronounced "children" with a long "i.")

I took her arm and propelled her firmly to a police box, always
handy in Japan. The report that Richi-san made there was long
and complicated, and interspersed with clipped "Ah, so?"s and "So
desu"s ("Isn't it so?") from the officer on duty. His imperturbability

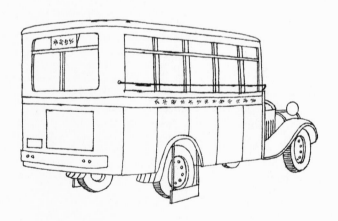

was reassuring, and soon Richi-san was smiling the way all Japanese do when recounting a misfortune.

"Papa-san," she said, "it was a free takushi. Not good idea, catching that kind. Cannot telephone company."

It took a moment for me to understand. A "free" cab was an independent cab.

The police put out an all-points bulletin. Two plain clothes men left on bicycles. I was restless enough to take another takushi-cab on another futile round. And meanwhile, the last bus of the afternoon left for Shizukawa.

Then Richi-san and little Masako-chan, both of them white-faced, and I made a long, slow cab trip through the streets of Sendai, still searching for Honorable Little Grandmother. The driver of this cab was both sympathetic and intelligent. He parked at each of the bus stations and went in to ask questions. At one of the stations, attendants remembered a little old lady, they told the driver, because she had an incredible amount of luggage. She had boarded a bus for Shizukawa.

This intelligence was not only heartening; it was almost beyond belief. How could Honorable Little Grandmother ever have managed to wrestle all that luggage into a bus? Only by the help of her takushi driver, whom I no longer remembered as a sinister-looking man but one obviously courteous and kind.

"But who bought her bus ticket?" I asked. "Who paid the cab? I must give her back the money she has spent."

Richi-san whirled on me. "What about *we're* money? Many takushis all over Sendai—maybe altogezzer one sousand yen we spend! *Never* I'm giving her back to money! Angree to her!"

Still indignant, she asked our cab driver the fare to follow the bus to Shizukawa, a considerable distance. He said four thousand yen, which is a little over eleven dollars. She said thirty-five hundred, and in the face of her wrath he quailed and said, "Dai jobu" ("All right"). The cab started off for Shizukawa.

I have had some wild taxi rides in various parts of the world, and a number of hair-raising experiences in Tokyo have made it perfectly clear to me why that city calls its cabs kamikaze takushis. But this was the wildest and most hazardous ride in my memory. The narrow road was unpaved and rough. It skirted cliffs in the mountains and clung precariously to high embankments in the water-filled lowlands, and darkness came soon after the ride began. Dust swirled into the back seat of the cab, and the tires banged large pebbles up onto the car's undersides. I am not built for such small "sid-downs," and through the two hours of our jolting pursuit my head kept bumping against the roof. At last, a few miles from Shizukawa, we caught up with the bus we thought Honorable Little Grandmother had boarded, and our driver flagged it down by halting his takushi squarely in the middle of the narrow road after a perilous passing. He hopped out into the swirling dust, and was at the bus door before I had unfolded myself from the rear seat.

When Richi-san, Masako-chan, and I reached the bus, we could see through the window that Honorable Little Grandmother was aboard, basking in the importance of having the takushi-cab driver stick his head in the door and page "Asano-san! Asano-san!" in the hearing of all the other passengers. We paid off our driver and got on the bus. There she sat, smiling, fat and happy and independent, surrounded by the luggage for which she had made herself responsible. Richi-san was too relieved and too tired to scold her then, and probably would not have done so in public, anyway. Besides, I thought I detected in Richi-san's smile a quiet pride. The scolding was to wait. . . .

THE CENTURIES SEEM TO HAVE PASSED SHIZUKAWA BY. IT IS A TILE- and thatch-topped town dreaming beside sun-washed Togura Bay, and Richi-san told me the name means "Clean Rivers." Landward are rolling hills and, beyond them, green mountains shouldering the sky. Flowering fields, green rice paddies, and fruitful orchards fill the valleys, but Shizukawa is chiefly a fishing town. Every morning, the boats skim out past the staked oyster beds of the inner bay, their engines chugging softly. Every day, they scatter beyond the verdant, surf-embroidered islands, getting their luck upon the sea much as the boats of Shizukawa did a thousand years ago. Every evening, they come chugging softly back to where lantern gleam ashore is reflected in the water. We heard them as we disembarked from the bus. "See, Papa-san!" Richi-san exclaimed, putting a hand to her ear. "I lovely that sound!"

My hotel had a poetic name having to do with a pine grove by the sea. There are three or four hotels in Shizukawa, but this one—managed by one of the Many Cousins of the Asano family—was the biggest and best situated. Honorable Little Grandfather's advance arrangements had provided me with a corner room on the second floor, overlooking the inevitable Japanese garden with its stone lanterns and goldfish pond, and the quiet, miniature beauty of Japanese gardens that never palls. Beyond this and across a country road—where I saw a milk goat being exercised by towing a man on a bicycle—were the pine trees, a community playground, and the blue-and-silver calm of the bay. I slept Japanese-style on futon under a tent-rigged mosquito netting, and in the morning the hotel supplied breakfast: one raw egg, two fried or scrambled eggs, fish, rice, pickles and miso-shiru, bean-curd soup. It doesn't take long to get accustomed to soup for breakfast, or even to like it. Each of the three mornings I was there, the elder grandchildren of the clan would arrive a few minutes after I had eaten, salute me by bowing low, with their knees and hands on the tatami mat, and chorus "Good-a morning, sir!" Then they would escort me along the waterfront, where fish nets were being mended and dried, and boats had been pulled out for repair, to the family home. There, without fail, I would be offered more fooding. And then Richi-san would introduce the subject of the day's puroguramu.

On the morning of the day before I had to leave she asked, "Papa-san, what you gonna doing today? Would you like somewhere pikunikku going on? Bee-cause pikunikku is Japanese custom."

"Picnics are also an American custom," I told her. "Let's go."

The family, it developed, had chartered a fishing boat, and in a

little while we boarded it, some ten or twelve of us. It was an ancient but graceful and seaworthy craft built of native cedar, about twenty feet long, and powered by a consumptive one-lunged engine. Its owner steered it, with magnificent aplomb, by means of a sweep oar. There were times when the coughing engine demanded the full attention of the one-man crew, but whenever a rock or shoal or some other obstruction appeared, and I was certain that we would run aground or foul the propeller in a string of fishing nets, he was always back manning the helm again.

Togura Bay is dotted with steep, pine-covered islands, and on one of them—Aoshima, or Green Island—we beached our boat in a rocky cove. The engine coughed and died. A flock of sea birds rose to wheel and cry, the gentle surf made music, and in the thick pines and the vine-tangled steepness overhanging the spray-wet rocks were thousands of suzumushi—Japanese singing insects that outdo songbirds. Nobody lives on Aoshima, and it was ours alone that day.

The tide went out, and the other men of the party—Honorable Little Grandfather, three uncles, and the boatman—immediately dispersed over the wet, shell-encrusted rocks to gather enough shellfish for a clambake in any language. Being unfamiliar with anything more exotic than simple bivalves, I could not help them, but I helped the children collect driftwood for the fire. Honorable Little Grandmother squatted among the rocks and boiled unshucked ears of corn in sea water; Richi-san and Ne-san (elder sister) shucked and buttered them. Honorable Little Grandmother also barbecued thin slices of chicken on a small grill, basting them with a sauce made of shoyu, sake, and sugar. The ten or more varieties of shellfish brought in by the foraging party were eaten both raw and cooked, among them tiny succulent awabi (abalone) no bigger than a small oyster; a spined sea urchin called uni, which resembles a chestnut bur and yields a light-brown meat that has a nutlike taste; hoya, a species of small clam that has become increasingly popular since Emperor Hirohito, who is world famous as an authority on marine biology, made a study of it. Unfortunately, there were no oysters. Richi-san explained, "Oysters don' have, Papa-san, because now making baby," and that reminded me that even in Japan there is no "r" in August, which is called Hachi-getsu, or "eighth month." Rice, sake, and biru topped off the menu.

In view of all this abundance it was difficult for me to understand why anybody had ever been worried about my fooding. I lay back on the rocks in the shade of the overhanging trees, smoking my pipe, listening to the bell, guitar, and violin tones of the singing insects, and watching a strange thing. Honorable Little Grandfather was pouring sake into a plastic jar holding about a pint of sea water and a dozen minnow-sized fish that the children had caught in nets. The volatile rice wine remained on top of the water, and the fish all stood on their tails and drank it, after which they became excessively lively, flopped out of their prison, and had to be recaptured from the rocks. Then Honorable Little Grandfather put fresh sea water into the jar, and for a while all the fish lay on the bottom in an abandoned stupor. But when they were returned to the sea, "so can growing up for eating," they all swam away energetically enough.

In midafternoon, we took to the boat again, and chugged out to the mouth of the bay to see Kami-wari and hear once more the story of how God cut open the rocks. Here the boatman pulled up a small pine seedling, and I learned that sake also has remarkable horticultural powers. He said he would plant the seedling in his garden and would pour a little sake around the roots several times a week to make it grow into a tree, strong and brave.

THAT EVENING, IN THE ANCESTRAL HOME, ON THE LAST DAY OF O-Bon, Richi-san finally spoke of what she called the "muchee troubling" caused by Honorable Little Grandmother at Sendai. The assembled clan listened, and Honorable Little Grandmother herself sat smiling inscrutably. Richi-san gave a full account of the takushi-cab mix-up, with emphasis on the worry it had caused other people and the number of yen it had cost. Seko-san, an uncle who is a painter and art teacher, nodded gravely and then commented at length. Richi-san translated for me.

The troubling was, Seko-san said, that now there were too many modern things. Too many takushi-cabs plying the streets of Sendai. Too many Basu Sentas; before, there had been only one in the city. "And he said the Number One bad sing"—Richi-san's voice rose to stress this—"is that O-baa-chan has bee-come a modern woman!"

This Number One badness of Honorable Little Grandmother was discussed for a long time there under the butsudan, or family altar, where the white paper lanterns burned softly and the ancestral spirits were gathered to listen. It is true that several adult members of the family smiled proudly and affectionately as they looked at O-baa-chan and nobody spoke a harsh word. But they all agreed that she had been very bad indeed in acting independently and causing anxiety to others. The grandchildren giggled openly. Every day of their young lives, they see some conflict between the old and the new, and they can understand and accept woman's new role in the social, economic, and political life of Japan, while the eldest sister cannot. Through it all, Honorable Little Grandmother sat like a plump Oriental statue, silent, smiling and serene. She *liked* being a modern woman.

Outside, the narrow streets of Shizukawa were brilliant with okuribi, the farewell fires lighted before all the houses to show the spirits the way back to the Meido, the unknown celestial world of darkness. Okuri-dango, or farewell rice balls, had been eaten, and others had been placed on the family altars.

O-Bon was almost over. It had been a good time, a happy time of prayer and feasting and rejoicing. That night's Bon-odori, or Dance of Rejoicing—a merry, graceful folk dance filled with hand-claps and posturings—brought young and old to the playground by the waterfront, and its drumbeat and flute shrill could be heard all over town. At midnight, each family gathered the okuri-dango that had been offered at the altars and reverently carried them to the waterfront. There, each family had a miniature boat made of rice straw, two or three feet long, and equipped with a rice-straw sail. The rice balls were placed aboard these boats to sustain the spirits on their outward journey. A small paper lantern lighted the bow of each miniature boat, while joss sticks burned fragrantly at the stern. An offshore breeze wafted the sacred Lilliputian fleet into the darkness of Togura Bay and on to the mysterious world of Meido.

The next morning, everybody but the youngest grandchild turned out at 4:30 to help me catch the bus for Sendai and to wave sayonara. The others from Tokyo were to stay on for a week or so. As the bus drove off, daylight began to show along the rough, narrow road, where pheasants whirred up out of the way-side grass as we passed, and from my seat by the window I could see in every waterway small straw boats, half sunk, their lantern lights gone out.

THE RICHI-SAN STORY

WHEN I HAD RETURNED TO JAPAN AFTER ALMOST A YEAR IN THE States, I thought I knew a little of the language and a lot about the customs. When I had tried most of the food, and had seen kabuki and Noh plays, and could give a takushi driver directions around Tokyo, or could drive to any part of the city myself—in short, when I had begun to fancy myself to be what the Navy used to call an Old China Hand—there was still one mystery that defied solution. This was Richi-san.

She had been my gaido, and even when O-jii-chan and O-baa-chan and some of the Many Cousins were with us, the interpretation of things Japanese still had to be hers, because of her charming English. She chattered brightly and musically most of the time, but never about herself. I remembered that when I first saw her I had thought she was perhaps seventeen. Now I had met Masako-chan, and it was obvious that Richi-san had to be considerably older to have such a daughter. I knew there was something more to her background than a country girl's upbringing. She was always very dainty and proper, and very consciously a lady. She did not have a large wardrobe of Western clothes, but what she wore was always tasteful, and she displayed excellent color sense. Once when we went to a movie in downtown Tokyo (she was mad about Bab Hopa, Geri Kupa, Dani Ke, and Tairon Pawa) she asked me to stop so she could buy a pair of white gloves. She had forgotten her gloves, and she gravely informed me that a lady never went anywhere—"must not anywhere going"—without them.

"I'm verree ba-ad head, Papa-san. I sink so."

"On the contrary, Richi-san, you have a very good head. You learn English fast."

"Papa-san oseji [flattery] speaking. Bee-fore time—you remember Sports Car Club?—I'm forget dictionary, and sun glasses, and camera. I sink somebody's house."

"Somebody's house?" I asked, bewildered.

"Yiss. Don' understand somebody's house, Papa-san?"

"No. I mean yes, I don't understand." (You have to be careful with negative questions. "No" to this one means you *do* understand.)

"Watsamatta you, Papa-san?" she asked impatiently. "Somebody's house!" She tapped her forehead. "Maybe nobody's house!"

"Oh," I said weakly. "You mean nobody home!"

That is a piece of slang from *circa* 1910, although Alexander Pope also used it long ago. I looked at Richi-san and knew she never possibly could have been around that long.

"Tell me, Richi-san—how old are you?"

She gave me a Mona Lisa smile. "Why you ask, Papa-san?"

"Oh, I'm just curious. How old?"

"I'm don' speaking how old. Never speaking!"

This, of course, was the eternal feminine, and I got nowhere. I could not learn Richi-san's age. She knew mine, which was very plainly advanced. I was an Honorable Elder, and she treated me with respect. We were teacher and pupil, and, although I never tried to tell her so, Richi-san was perhaps the daughter I never had.

I think it is certain that if I had not gone to the States and come

back to Japan the second time I would never have known her
story. . . .

IT MAY WELL BE THAT ALL AMERICAN NAVAL OFFICERS IN JAPAN
suffer from a traditional heritage, and one entirely fictional, which
the Japanese keep alive and even cherish, because they love sad
stories. The American naval officers may all be Pinkertons, straight
from *Madame Butterfly*. It is well known that they sail away, and
the "one fine day" of their returning never comes.

I can easily imagine what the Japanese fondness for Puccini has
done to hamper romance. Everybody in Japan knows the sad story
of Cho-cho-san; Japanese slang has adopted the word *butterfry*. A
butterfry is a fickle person, one who flits from flower to flower, and
the term is used for either sex. Unfortunately, the same philosophy
applies in some measure to friendships. The Japanese friend seldom
lets down his natural and formidable reserve. The American friend
sails away. He writes a few times, and often gifts are exchanged;
then the correspondence becomes desultory, and dies. That is the
end.

I was the exception. *I* came back. In returning to Japan, I attained a degree of permanency in the hearts and minds of the
Asano family, and in those of many other Japanese who had been
nothing more than casual acquaintances. They treated me more
warmly. America was no longer a million miles across the Pacific:
if I had returned to Japan once, I could do so again.

Nothing much had changed. Goto-san had a better job. O-jii-
chan, carefully saving his money, had not yet found a place to
build a house. Kyobashi Cousin and her husband were unhappily
talking about getting what Richi-san called a "ree-vorce." Richi-san
was talking about how well Masako-chan was doing in school, and
in her piano and dancing lessons. She was considering some kind
of "small busy-ness" that would make more money than she was
earning sewing kimono. "Bee-cause," she said, "if I don' work, my
baby don' eat."

She was sitting on the tatami in the Ogu-machi apato, cutting squares of material that looked like unbleached muslin and sewing them on a portable Japanese sewing machine. I asked her what she was making.

"Zabuton [cushion] cover, Papa-san," she said.

"But I never saw a zabuton covered with that kind of material. They are always pretty and bright, and usually covered with silk."

"Different, Papa-san—is different. This zabuton cover making for my grandmuzzer, living in Miyagi-ken. You don' meet my grandmuzzer. Verree old 'oman—maybe ninety-five years old—almost dead. Every day, must u-ashing her zabuton covers. Bee-cause, Papa-san," she added with perfect innocence, "she's all time just a little pee. Can't be helped."

It's a universal word, I have noticed, and I managed not to smile. "I see," I said. "Your family is very long-lived. I mean you live to an old age. You will live to be a very old woman, I think."

The Mona Lisa smile. "Already old 'oman, Papa-san."

"That," I said, "is tondemonai, or what we call ridiculous. Of course, you never told me your age. But you could pass Masako-chan for your kid sister instead of your daughter. You could say you are twenty. You didn't keep your husband's name after he died, Richi-san. Is that a Japanese custom?"

"No, Papa-san—not Japanese custom. I'm keeping fazzer's name bee-cause first ree-vorce, then husband dead after ree-vorce. Zo-o, I'm changee name back to Asano. Verree sorree, before don' telling you. But I'm bashful, su-peaking zose sings. And I'm sinking just *my* busy-ness."

"I apologize," I said. "It certainly is just your business. It was very rude of me to ask."

Richi-san put aside her sewing. "Not rude, Papa-san. I will tell-ing you, now. My old—I am old 'oman, Papa-san. Thirty-seven yu-ears old."

"What? Tondemonai!"

"Yiss, Papa-san. Tu-rue—it's tu-rue." She began wiping her eyes as if mourning her lost youth, and she still looked like a child.

"Sid-down, Papa-san, and I will telling you verree sad story. Please don' speaking this story to my fazzer and muzzer, bee-cause many sings I don' tell to them. Understand, Papa-san?"

"I understand," I said.

RICHI-SAN WAS BORN AT THE FAMILY HOME IN SHIZUKAWA, WHERE we had gone for O-Bon. She was the youngest of O-jii-chan's children, and he was a man of substance and standing in the community, operating a four-chair barbershop on the ground floor of the big home at the principal intersection; he had the first telephone in town, and the first radio. The Asano children were brought up in an atmosphere of love, and were well sheltered and well fed. There were many relatives living in Shizukawa in those days; the family ties were strong. Richi-san's elder brother went off to the university when she was just a child. She attended middle school, studied piano and sewing and sketching; she played happily in the pine grove by the waterfront, and there were picnics and beach outings. She remembers her earlier school years, when Japanese militarism was ascendant. Every morning she bowed with all the other pupils before a portrait of the August One, the Emperor, and sang a song that said:

> Boku wa gunjin dai-suki yo;
> Ima ni o-kiku natta nara,
> Kun-sho sagete, ken-tsutte,
> Onma ni notte kae-ro ka!

(In this, the word *onma* is derived from *o-uma* or "honorable horse" and the prefix "o" is not only an honorific, but is used to sound more childish. In this case its use may mean either or both.)

> I love a soldier, very, very much;
> When I grow up,
> Decorations on chest and saber at belt,
> To my home town I want to return on horseback!

The song was recruiting propaganda, and no doubt its singing all over Japan produced future soldiers—but it did not inspire Richi-san. Her family was strongly Nicheren Buddhist by religion; they abhorred all forms of violence. They never spanked their children, nor even raised their voices to correct them. Besides, Richi-san was being carefully reared to serve only two masters—Kami (God) and her husband.

The mold was precious in those prewar days, in the provinces of Japan that were still virtually untouched by foreign mores, and it cast a shining product. Lafcadio Hearn, who was there seventy years before I came, wrote a love letter to all Japanese women in his *Japan: an Attempt at Interpretation,* generally acknowledged to be his best work. It was his last book on Japan, and it expressed his disillusionment in many things, but these did not include the Japanese woman. He became maudlin, it is true, and still he said it better than I can say:

> . . . the most wonderful aesthetic products of Japan are not its ivories, nor its bronzes, nor its porcelains, nor its swords, nor any of its marvels in metal or lacquer— but its women. Accepting as partly true the statement that woman everywhere is what man has made her, we might say that this statement is more true of the Japanese woman than of any other. Of course it required thousands and thousands of years to make her; but the period of which I am speaking beheld the work completed and perfected. Before this ethical creation, criticism should hold its breath, for there is here no single fault save the fault of a moral charm unsuited to any world of selfishness and struggle. . . . Perhaps no such type of woman will appear again in this world for a hundred thousand years: the conditions of industrial civilization will not admit of her existence. The type could not have been created in any society shaped on modern lines . . . it has no more in common with the humanity of this twentieth century of ours—perhaps very much less—than has

the life depicted upon old Greek vases. Its charm is the charm of a vanished world—a charm strange, alluring, indescribable as the perfume of some flower of which the species became extinct in our Occident before the modern languages were born. . . . With the Japanese woman, as formed by the ancient training, each act of life was an act of faith: her existence was a religion, her home a temple, her every word and thought ordered by the law of the cult of the dead. . . . This wonderful type is not extinct, though surely doomed to disappear. A human creature so shaped for the services of gods and men that every beat of her heart is duty, that every drop of her blood is moral feeling, were not less out of place in the future world of competitive selfishness, than an angel in hell.

THOSE WERE THE STRONG WORDS OF A MAN DRUNK WITH SENTIment and with his own power to use words, and yet much of what Hearn wrote was true in his time, and some of it is true today. Many may wonder how a barber's children could be reared under such high ideals, but Shizukawa was a remote place, and ruled by the old ways; and in the old times an artisan was highly respected. Richi-san, brought up to honor and serve the elders in her family, lived in a lovely little world which she thought could never change. The seasons in Shizukawa are a parade of beauty: spring brings plum trees white as snow, and pink cherry bloom marching softly over the gentle slopes of the lower hills; summer is a delight of surf-embroidered beaches and fruitful orchards and fields, and autumn's torch sets the maple-covered mountains on fire. The winters are mild by the sea, but the higher places are beautifully mantled in white. And along with the seasons go the festivals— o-matsuri—rich in prayer and pageantry, costume and feasting, all marked on the ancient lunar calendar. It was a life that asked little of the outside world, and perhaps gave nothing except beauty to be seen and heard; it was a patterned life, regimented by custom

and precept and the traditions of centuries, and channeled by them into ordered confines. But it was happy and secure, until the militarists destroyed it, along with everything else that was Old Japan. . . .

Richi-san reached a marriageable age just before the war. Her elder brother had known a personable and promising young fellow student at the university, a graduate who had gone to work for the Japanese National Railways in their new field—China. The two kept up a correspondence, and one day the brother sent his friend a snapshot of Richi-san. It was taken on a festival day when she was nineteen, and nineteen is often the time of a Japanese girl's first blossoming. She wore her Number One kimono, and was happy, and beautiful. To the young man in far-off Tientsin, the picture symbolized all that was lovely in his homeland, and for him it was love at first sight. He asked the brother to serve as nakodo—the traditional go-between—and months later he returned to Japan for what is called omiai, the first meeting of prospective bride and bridegroom.

The meeting was brief, and formal. Nobody asked Richi-san, and, reared as she had been, she could not question the arrangements. The parents on both sides were convinced it would be a good match. It was not rushed: the young man went back to China, to return later. There finally came a day when Richi-san wore a new kimono, and the bride's white hat which comes down over the forehead to conceal the horns of jealousy. It was on a day of kichi-jitsu—a day of good luck—by the lunar calendar. Before the assembled relatives of both, the betrothed each vowed to be faithful, one to the other, and each drank sacred wine from three cups, three times, in san-san-kudo, or "three times three" ritual. And so they were wed.

At the reception which followed, everybody was careful not to speak the word *sayonara,* which means parting, and brings bad luck. But the husband had to go back to China just one week after the ceremony, and Richi-san, after the custom, was now his mother's daughter. She would live at the home of his parents in Tokyo.

She did not know what had happened, only a few months before, in this house. There had been a daughter of Richi-san's age— in fact, the resemblance between the two girls was remarkable— who had been similarly pledged in marriage. Secretly and hopelessly, she was already in love with another man. . . .

"Zo-o, Papa-san," Richi-san related sadly, "she's killing she-self— dead. Verree sad, that killing; I'm sorree to her. But her muzzer, Papa-san, maybe *not* sorree. Just angree. Verree strangee 'oman, my husband's muzzer, and verree strong heart!"

The mother-in-law had insisted upon her daughter's marriage, and now she may have blamed herself for the suicide. She was tormented by a feeling of guilt, and every time she looked upon the face of her new daughter-in-law, she saw the child she had lost. Her "strong heart" turned bitter and cold toward Richi-san, who was doing her utmost to please.

"Papa-san, I was verree bad time, that house! Just like servant—maybe same-same maid-san. Too muchee cleaning and u-ashing sings, and not enough fooding. Just one handful rice every day, nossing more. I'm all time verree hungree, and verree skinny—almost like to dead, like being dead. One yu-ear I'm staying that house, Papa-san, before China going. But I don' send letter to my fazzer and muzzer speaking zose sings. Bee-cause, Papa-san, Japanese wife must never speaking that kind sings about husband or husband's family. Zo-o, I was don' speak."

Finally, reduced to a skeleton by starvation and hard work, Richi-san was summoned to join her husband in Tientsin. Just before this journey, the Japanese militarists had extended their adventures to a place called Pearl Harbor. . . .

O-JII-CHAN (HIS ELDER SON HAD ONLY RECENTLY CONFERRED THE title of Honorable Little Grandfather upon him by presenting him with a granddaughter) was at work in his barber-shop in Shizukawa when the radio brought the news. No war would have been of O-jii-chan's choosing, but, like millions of other Japanese, he had no voice in the matter. He was sad, and knew misgivings, but he also was patriotic. He went upstairs to O-baa-chan and to the family shrine, and to both he made his report: the glorious armies of the Emperor were fighting in a new place, and doing very well.

Then the Asanos of Shizukawa settled down to a war that touched them only a little, compared to what happened in Tokyo and in other industrial centers. They almost always had enough to eat, enjoying the many varieties of shellfish taken from the picturesque rocks around Togura Bay. Deep-sea fishing was necessarily greatly reduced, but the shellfish were nearby, and anybody could catch tako, or octopus, simply by lowering earthenware pots into the harbor during the cold months. Sugar was hard to get, but salt was even more scarce throughout most of Japan, and the people of Shizukawa turned that scarcity to profit: they made salt by evaporating sea water, then took it inland and traded it to the farmers for eggs, poultry, and vegetables. There were a few alarms and excursions around Togura Bay—somebody had pointed out on the map that the southern arm of the bay, where Kami-wari stands, is the nearest point of land in Japan to the west coast of America, and therefore the Americans were sure to launch an attack against that sector of Miyagi Prefecture.

This was nothing but barber-chair strategy. Except for Sendai, a considerable distance over the mountains to the south, there were no targets of military importance. One day a large ship (a carrier) stood off the entrance to the bay and launched some of its aircraft, and these made a great business of machine-gunning the staked oyster beds close inshore. O-jii-chan rumbles with infectious laughter when he tells about this, and says he believes the American pilots mistook the rows of stakes for a mine field. In one other case, he says, airplanes strafed a small place being used for a hospital, but not marked with a red cross, probably because the pilots thought it was a small factory. Nobody was hurt, but the hospital personnel fled into a nearby rice paddy and fell face down in the mud. This struck O-jii-chan and O-baa-chan as something like slapstick comedy.

But one thing worried them. Richi-san's letters from China became fewer and fewer, and finally stopped altogether. They did not know whether she was dead or alive.

Down in Tokyo, Shinjuku Aunt and Unc' were not quite so fortunate. They saw all the many bombings of that city, and finally their own house was destroyed. It was not struck by a bomb, but was burned by a spreading fire, and they had time to save many of their effects. Nor were they ever really hungry. When the war began, Shinjuku Unc' showed his foresight—and his lack of sympathy with the conflict—by becoming a hoarder of the first magnitude. Shrewdly, he bought all the miso (soybean paste) he could get his hands on. Miso is rich in protein; it makes delicious and nutritious soup. Shinjuku Aunt and Unc' had enough to last them through the war. It was after the surrender that they began to suffer a little. They had to resort to kaidashi (foraging) by going to the country and trading with farmers. Many a farmer's wife turned out in expensive and rich kimono in those days, through barter. The people of burned-out Tokyo, trading their clothing for food, were said to be living a takenoko existence. The word translates "bamboo skin" or "onion skin" life—literally, peeling the skin off the bamboo. . . .

IT WAS PERHAPS JUST AS WELL THAT O-JII-CHAN AND O-BAA-CHAN did not hear from Richi-san during her last couple of years in China. She was more dead than alive.

Tientsin was bombed only once, as she remembers it, and her war was a different kind—heartbreak, starvation, and disease. Her husband had changed since that brief and tender week of their honeymoon in Tokyo; he had become a gambler, and in the old tradition of railroad men everywhere, he spent a lot of time away from home.

"I sink maybe his muzzer writing to him ba-ad letters about me," Richi-san said. "Before, maybe good heart, he had. But in China, was verree ba-ad heart. Why, I don' know."

Whatever the reason, her husband did not leave her enough money, and she went hungry. And now she was pregnant. Chinese neighbors shared their meager food with her, or she would have died then. Nobody had enough to eat. Richi-san was lucky to get another handful of rice per day. The baby came, and she had no milk for it, and after a month it died.

There was no escape. Her training had been absolute. She had been taught—and she believed it—that if a marriage failed the wife was to blame. It was the wife's task to obey, blindly and uncomplainingly, and to accept her lot as cheerfully as she could. So Richi-san wrote nothing of complaint to her parents—the letters probably would not have gone through anyway—and her only solace was in praying to Buddha. She will listen to no criticism of the Chinese, now, because the Chinese were kind to her. But nobody had any food. . . .

Another child was born in the summer of 1945, and Richi-san fell desperately ill of pleurisy and pneumonia, aggravated by a long period of malnutrition. For years she had been suffering from what the Japanese call kakke, or beri-beri, an ailment caused by an insufficiency of certain vitamins. Her husband was not with her. He had been home only a few times. When he appeared—usually drunk—he had already lost all his pay at gambling, and was there to demand that Richi-san give him the preciously small sum she had managed to hoard for food. Even when her illness became grave, he refused to take her to the hospital. Once again, her Chinese neighbors helped her, and cared for the sick baby as best they could while she spent more than a month in a dirty and wretchedly overcrowded hospital in Tientsin. The food there was not much better, and she almost died. This was in that fateful August of 1945.

On July 26, the Allies' Potsdam Declaration had called upon the Japanese to surrender unconditionally, and three days later the Japanese militarists rejected that demand. None of this news sifted down to Richi-san, in China; nor did the news of the world's first atomic bomb, which fell on Hiroshima on August 6. But she did hear—on August 9—that Russia had declared war on Japan, and she gave no thought to the opportunistic and belated nature of that act: she and all the other Japanese in China were only frightened by the news.

The Russians were coming. Richi-san's husband feared them as much as anybody else, and he came for her. She got out of bed, hardly able to stand.

That day they heard a dramatic and historical broadcast from Japan. It was the voice of the August One—the Emperor. It had never before been heard on the radio, and she remembers it. All through the morning of August 15 (it was August 14 in America) the Tokyo radio told its audience to listen to the Emperor's broadcast at noon.

Trains stopped all over Japan so that passengers could hear the message from loudspeakers on the station platforms. In China, the Japanese stood by.

At twelve o'clock Emperor Hirohito told his eighty-three million subjects—in a voice they had never heard before, but one revered as would have been the voice of God—that the war was over.

RICHI-SAN AND HER HUSBAND AND BABY TOOK A TRAIN FROM TIENT-sin to Tansan. This was a short distance: the journey normally required only one hour. But Chiang Kai-shek's troops had dynamited the track in many places, and it took them two days to get to Tansan. Both Richi-san, and the baby were pitifully sick.

They stayed in Tansan for four months during the fearful chaos that followed the Surrender. What was left of the Japanese Army in China was in charge, and this was fortunate. Food was rationed —there was not much of it, but Richi-san got her meager share. Most of the Japanese refugees lived in cold, barnlike barracks, but because of her illness she was favored with a two-and-one-half-mat room—a room perhaps six by seven feet. There were not enough blankets to keep her and the baby warm. Richi-san was skin and bones, weighing perhaps seventy pounds, and the baby had no chance to live. They were waiting . . . waiting . . . waiting . . . and for what they did not know.

Finally they were moved again, to Tanku, which was a seaport. And then: "Then, Papa-san, one day—oh, verree cold day, maybe almost Kurisumasu [Christmas]—was coming American ship. What kind ship, I don' know. But I sink was Navy ship."

I drew a rough sketch of an LST. Richi-san wiped away her tears, and studied it a moment.

"Yiss, yiss—that kind ship, Papa-san! Was too many people going that ship—maybe three sousand people. Verree happee, bee-cause going back to Japan. But was too muchee crowded. People cannot going inside ship, just on top, and was u-raining and verree cold wezzer. Cannot lying down for sleeping, just stand-upping or some-time sid-down little while. Six days we staying that ship, Papa-san. Ba-ad—was verree bad. Everybody too muchee cold, and cannot fooding that many people. Zo-o, just verree thin rice, same-same soup. And Papa-san?"

"Yes, Richi-san?"

"My baby almost dead—was almost dead—and I'm almost dead too. But was American man—'hat you say, sailor? Yiss, I sink sailor —Navy sailor. Bee-cause, I remember, that time was first time I'm seeing Navy unihorm—blue unihorm and white hat. He's speaking to me, Papa-san, and I'm verree su'pris*ed*. He don' speak ozzer people, three sousand people. Why, Papa-san?"

"Why? I don't know why. But I think if I saw you in a crowd, with a sick baby—yes, I think I know why. But what happened?"

"I don' know that speaking, bee-cause I don' English. Just one word, I understand—'baby.' I sink maybe was speaking 'Your baby sick, please giving to baby this food.' And, Papa-san, he's pu-resent me egg—oh, verree prettee fresh egg—and chocolate, two pieces."

Richi-san was smiling, now, reliving a moment when someone was kind to her. She wiped away her tears, and she looked very young. There were no wrinkles in her face, and her hair was as black as a crow's wing. She did not look thirty-seven—much less like a woman of thirty-seven who had borne three children, and lost two of them, and had experienced four years of starvation and illness and tragedy.

She said, "Every day, Papa-san, he's bringing me zose kind sings. My baby was too small, and too sick—baby cannot eating zose sings, that kind fooding. Zo-o, I'm eating. I sink if not that fooding, I'm dead— I would being dead!"

The LST reached Sasebo after a stormy passage, and they were disembarked. American Army medical authorities took one look at Richi-san and her baby and put them in another overcrowded hospital. It was too late: the baby died that night. But the food was heavenly to Richi-san. After a week of good food and rest and nursing care, she was strong enough to go on to Tokyo by rail. She remembers that her husband's overcoat was stolen, that night, on the train. . . .

HER ORDEAL WAS NOT OVER. ONCE MORE SHE LIVED WITH HER husband's mother, and once more she was not welcome in that house. Food was very scarce in postwar Tokyo, and she was given

only scraps. But her letters to her parents indicated that all was well
—it would not have been proper to write otherwise. Masako-chan
was born a year later, when conditions had improved slightly, and
when she was a few months old Richi-san took her to Shizukawa.
O-jii-chan, usually the mildest of men, exploded in wrath when he
saw his emaciated daughter.

"Fazzer was verree angree. He was tol' me, 'if you stay with that
man, you will dead—will being dead!' Zo-o, I don' go back to the
Tokyo. I'm staying in Shizukawa. Fazzer and Muzzer keeping
Masako-chan their house for maybe one yu-ear, and I'm living in
Buddhist place [a Buddhist temple], just pu-raying Buddha all
time—every day, pu-raying long time. Then, Papa-san, I'm ree-
vorce."

Divorce was a rather new and strange thing in Japan, and Richi-
san took the step reluctantly. She and her parents knew that, along
with hundreds of thousands of war widows her age, her chances of
remarriage were slim. They also felt that if she went back to her
husband she would die. She resumed her maiden name, and slowly
regained her health.

"Did you have good food, in the Buddhist place?"

"Not good food, Papa-san. Was verree poor place. Just boiled ika
[squid] and-a o-mugi [barley], not rice—rice, don' have. But was
quiet place, Papa-san."

Richi-san needed a quiet place, and meditation and prayer. She
occupied herself sewing kimono, and earned a little money selling
them. Little Masako-chan became the favorite grandchild in the
Asanos' ancestral home, and when Richi-san finally was strong
enough to go to Tokyo to look for a job—"bee-cause Shizukawa was
like dead town, Papa-san—never growing"—she had to leave the
baby behind. "If I'm taking her to the Tokyo, Papa-san Fazzer and
Muzzer too muchee cry-cry."

I knew the rest of the story, and was silent, and almost ashamed.
It is hard to say why. We Americans did not bring about the
tragedy of the war, and during those four years the Japanese were
our enemies—and I hated them as fervently as any patriotic Amer-

ican hated them. But people like the Asanos did not bring about the war either; and we were never at war with small, gentle, defenseless women, or with hungry babies. And, all the time, we had so much of food and warmth. . . .

"Papa-san?"

"Yes, Richi-san?"

"Some time I 'ant again meeting that American Navy man. I 'ant to telling him, 'Kindly to me, sank you verree muchee, beecause that kind fooding fresh eggs and chocolate saving my life.' You understand, Papa-san?"

"I understand."

"You will please helping me find that Navy man, Papa-san? I 'ant verree muchee!"

"I will try," I said.

And maybe I can help find him. Maybe he will read this, and remember, and come forward to identify himself. I have nothing to go by, except what Richi-san told me, out of her heart. He could have been a hospital corpsman, or a ship's cook, or one of the deck force able to "cumshaw" fresh eggs from the galley and buy chocolates from the small ship's store. Whatever his name or rating, I like him, and I like to think that he was a true American and a true Navy man—and yet his choice must have been heartbreakingly difficult. Because he could not supply everybody with special food, and out of three thousand people there must have been many others who were hungry and ill.

I should like to ask him why he went to Richi-san, out of the three thousand, with his very pretty fresh egg and his chocolate, two pieces, that very first time. Having done it once, he would have to do it again. And I think perhaps I know why he did it the first time. I think that even at death's door Richi-san had something proud and unconquerable in her eyes, and with it, perhaps, the light of her shining faith in Buddha.

I should like to thank him, too, for knowing Richi-san and her family has been one of the most enriching things in my own life.

SEVEN

THE KOKUTERU HOUSE

THE MEMBERS OF THE IMMEDIATE ASANO FAMILY ARE ALL DEVOUT and practicing Nichiren Buddhists, with the possible exception of O-baa-chan. Hers is a strangely independent spirit, considering the times and the customs of her more than seventy years. She must have been lovely when she was young—a time when a Japanese wife was literally the "Honorable Person of the Interior," existing only to serve her husband and her family. Now O-baa-chan's hair has thinned and is slightly gray, and when she stoops to household tasks O-jii-chan laughs fondly and remarks that her legs remind him of daikon, the big white radish that grows three feet long in Japan. But O-baa-chan's eyes are bright and laughter becomes her, and she sometimes gives way to a prankish irreverence in religious matters. I suspect that it amuses her to talk, giggle, or bang pots and pans together while other people are at their daily hour-long devotions. Once I observed O-jii-chan at prayer in the Ogu-machi apato. He knelt before a small family altar with its greenery and lighted candles, he rang a tinkling hand bell, and was not at all abashed by the presence of a Christian as he chanted "Namu-myo-ho-renge-kyo!" over and over, through a full range of intonations. Because of failing eyesight, he was using a large reading glass on his Nichiren prayer book. Holding the glass made it impossible for him to rub his prayer beads in the accustomed manner, and this sent O-baa-chan—the Modern U-oman—into irrepressible giggles.

O-baa-chan liked attention, and it may be that she was only trying to attract it when she did such things. Certainly it was the collective faith of all the members of the household that sustained them that winter, when the acute housing shortage in Tokyo forced them out of the apato before they were ready to move.

All of Japan was still short of housing. Tokyo, burned out during the war by the fire raids, and skyrocketing to a population of nearly nine million, lacked several hundred thousand housing units. All over the city were families of five or six huddled into single "six-mat" rooms, or even smaller spaces of four mats. A tatami mat is three feet wide and six feet long, so that a four-mat room is seventy-two square feet. Kyobashi Cousin, with her husband and small son, had only four mats, and perhaps this was a contributing factor to the threatened "ree-vorce." Shinjuku Aunt and Unc' had a larger home and a bigger family, and crowded themselves by taking in several college students as boarders. Even under such cramped conditions the living spaces—uncluttered by furniture—were always clean and neat.

O-jii-chan, O-baa-chan, Richi-san, and Masako-chan were much better off than most of their Tokyo relatives. The Ogu-machi apato was behind a fish store. It consisted of an eight-mat room, a six-mat room, and community kitchen privileges in the hall, with a single gas burner for their individual use, a private storage bin for vegetables under the hall floor, and the right to use the community sink's cold water. Crude toilet facilities were shared with the fish-store crew, and daily baths could be had at the public bathhouse at a cost of three or four cents for each person.

Poor as the Asanos were, they understood and took advantage of electrical appliances far more than the average Japanese family did at that time. In the last three years, the appliance business has enjoyed a tremendous boom in Japan, but when the Asanos lived in Ogu-machi possession of such household aids was unusual. With O-jii-chan's eldest son in the book and radio business, they could buy appliances at wholesale prices, and they had a small electric washing machine, a record player, a radio, a steam iron, a toaster, a hot plate, and even a terebi (television set). In a neighborhood where terebi were owned only by restaurants and o-sushi bars, this gave them distinction and brought hordes of Masako-chan's first-grade schoolmates to the apato every evening.

But these things took up room, and the matter of space also was complicated by the household's love for pets. They could not resist the appeal of small creatures—furred, feathered, scaled, or plated. At the time they were anxiously looking for land on which to build they had in residence a short-tailed kitten named Tami-chan, two quarrelsome parakeets, a kanariya (canary) brought from Shizukawa which could "verree pretty songing;" a goldfish tank containing —Richi-san said—"twelve people"; a tureen-sized turtle which made fearful armorial clankings in trying to scale the walls of its washtub; four white Leghorn baby chicks Masako-chan had acquired at school; and a mongrel puppy named John. As if this menagerie were not enough, Richi-san was casting covetous eyes at a small monkey she had seen in the neighborhood. It was, she said, "almost like somebody."

I had not seen John, who was kept under the outside stairs that led to the second floor, when first I heard her delighted announcement that a puppy had been added to the collection.

"Boy dog, I hope," I told Richi-san.

"Oh, yiss, I sink so," she answered. "And, Papa-san, verree good head. Smart head, that puppydog!"

"Well, that's good. But you're getting an awful lot of pets for such a small place, you know."

"Oh, yiss. We must new house making, Papa-san. But now so many don' have. Bee-cause last week two people dead. Was dead."

"Two people dead? What kind of people?"

"Goldfish, Papa-san. Verree sorree to them. We was praying to Buddha."

I expressed my sympathy for the departed, but pointed out that two fewer people in the goldfish tank in no way alleviated the space problem. Tami-chan, once a playful kitten, had begun ranging by night. The four White Leghorns all turned out to be roosters and woke the neighborhood at dawn with their cock-a-doodle-do, which the Japanese call kokekokko. John bayed the moon, and the family was reminded of a kotawaza, or proverb, which was translated to me as, "If one dog speaks, many dogs speaking." The parakeets grew more quarrelsome daily, and the Asanos had a humorous theory about their incompatibility: it very probably was caused, they said with a tolerant smile, by the atomic fallout.

Although the government of Japan officially viewed the many atomic and H-bomb tests that year more seriously, there were many popular jokes about the menace: in o-sushi bars the Japanese playfully inquired whether or not the tasty raw fish was gembaku no maguro—atom-bombed tuna. But hat stores did a thriving business, because it was widely believed that radioactive rain and dust would lead to a condition called tako nyudo, or bald as an octopus. . . .

However, the tests went on in the Pacific, and were being conducted somewhere behind the Iron Curtain. Prevailing winds in Japan come from the west; Japanese scientists always knew when the Soviets had touched off a nuclear explosion in Siberia. If it was no time to be bareheaded, it certainly was not a time to be without a roof, and after a visit from the "fish-store master" who owned the apato, the Asanos quite suddenly found themselves facing that probability.

The fish store had not been profitable, the owner explained. He was going to close it and devote his full attention to the bigger fish store he operated a few blocks away, and he had leased the Ogu-machi space to a family that planned to open a Chinese noodle restaurant. This family would have to live in, as do most Japanese shopkeepers; therefore, the Asanos' apato had been included in the deal. With many apologies, the owner gave them three months' notice.

Everybody had been vainly hunting "ground" for many months.

I had driven Richi-san to dozens of places, and sometimes we took O-jii-chan along, only to meet disappointment. It seemed that the newspapers never advertised anything but land suitable for business use; one heard of residential lots only by word of mouth or from neighborhood real estate offices. Nobody had to advertise. Land in the Tokyo area was not only scarce but, judging by the price, it might have been paved with gold so far as the Asanos were concerned. Prices were going up all the time. The absolute minimum seemed to be fifteen thousand yen—more than forty dollars—per tsubo, and that was in swamp or slum areas; in modestly better districts the price ran to fifty thousand yen or more. A tsubo is roughly the equivalent of two tatami mats, or thirty-six square feet; it takes about a hundred tsubo to make what we would call an average city lot.

I was forced to inquire into the state of O-jii-chan's finances, because I found myself in the role of respected family adviser. He had managed to save some money during his long years as the Number One barber in Shizukawa, and he had a small income in rentals from his two sons, who were occupying his property there.

"How much has he saved?" I asked.

O-jii-chan had almost eight hundred thousand yen—more than two thousand dollars. In Japan, where a carpenter will work a long day for a dollar, a house can be built for that. But it will not buy a piece of ground in Tokyo.

"What are you going to do?" I asked Richi-san when I heard about the three-month notice from the fish-store master.

"We will praying to Buddha, Papa-san," she said.

It is a curious thing to me that in the many times I have heard the Asano's long and fervent prayers to Buddha there never seemed to be any deviation from the chant of "Glory to the Supreme Law of the Lotus!" that could be taken as any special supplication. As far as I could tell, they made no mention in their prayers of a house or lot—but they prayed longer and more frequently. After the notice from the fish-store master, they alarmed me by becoming completely passive in their attitude; they no longer even spoke of "ground," nor did they ask me to drive them anywhere in search of it. But they began, for the first time, to study house plans.

"Papa-san, you sink making kokuteru house good idea?" Richi-san asked me one day in September, when nearly three weeks of their notice had elapsed.

"Kokuteru house? What's that? Oh—a cocktail house!" For a moment, I thought the Asanos were planning to open a small cocktail lounge. But then I remembered that kokuteru is a word they use for a blend of anything—in architecture or fashions as well as in drinks. It is a mixture.

"Yiss, you knows—kokuteru sutairu [cocktail style]. Maybe Western-sutairu living room and kitchen, and frush toilet—flush toilet. Ozzer sings Japanese."

I said weakly that maybe a kokuteru house was a good idea, but first—*what about the land?*

Richi-san said, with the faith of centuries, "Papa-san don' u-orry about it. Buddha will taking care to us."

And she and O-jii-chan went to the family altar to pray again.

On my next weekly visit to the Ogu-machi apato, Richi-san was in high spirits. She greeted me with "Papa-san, you will being verree su'pris*ed!* Day before yesterday we buying some ground. Oh, verree prettee place, I sink so!"

It seemed that for the first time a newspaper advertisement had announced the sale of residential lots. They were in a subdivision of Totsuka, a suburb within the city limits of Yokohama, just twenty-eight miles from Tokyo. The price was three thousand yen per tsubo. Honorable Little Grandfather had answered the advertisement and had bought a lot of a hundred and twenty-five tsubo.

To the Asanos this sudden turn in their fortunes was not at all surprising. Buddha, they said, had answered their prayers.

I drove out to see the lot the next day, with Richi-san as my gaido. It was a well-favored site, with excellent bus and train facilities. Located on high ground just east of the busy Tokaido Highway, Japan's Route 1, it commanded a lovely view of a checkerboard farming valley that changes color with the seasons, and majestic Fuji-san could be seen to the southwest. Sixteen pine trees fringed the lot, and Richi-san had already named the place Sixteen Pines. The transaction had taken almost half of O-jii-chan's bank account, but the family was undismayed: "Buddha will taking care to us."

Back in Tokyo, telephone calls went out to various construction companies. Their representatives came to the apato on bicycles, carrying briefcases stuffed with brochures and finance plans—all of them exorbitant.

I did not see how the Asanos could afford to build the house but, after learning the price he had to pay for land, O-jii-chan had raised something more than two hundred thousand yen from his two sons. And now O-baa-chan also came to his aid, and Richi-san proudly told me about it:

"Papa-san, you knows what means o-fukuro? Many yu-ears ago, Japanese people calling muzzer that name. Bee-cause she's all time keeping sings in sack—maybe needle and thread, maybe money. Zo-o, sometimes don' tell family about money. Understand, Papa-san?"

"O-fukuro—Honorable Bag?" I said.

"Yiss, was calling muzzer of family that name. O-baa-chan was keeping money. Few days ago she's giving Fazzer that money for making house. He's verree happee!"

I never learned just how many thousand yen O-baa-chan had managed to hoard during the years as keeper of the family purse, but it helped. O-jii-chan's total capital now stood at about seven hundred and fifty thousand yen. But the building companies all wanted at least a million yen to construct a house of modest size. They would take seven hundred thousand from O-jii-chan, and build the house; they required what amounted to a first mortgage on the property for the remaining three hundred thousand—to be paid off in monthly installments over a period of seven years. I could not fully understand the interest rates, but it was apparent that in borrowing three hundred thousand yen from the building company the Asanos would have to pay back almost six hundred thousand. Over innumerable cups of honorable tea, deals were discussed and house plans studied.

"Papa-san," Richi-san said one day as she scanned a floor plan, "what you sink about interest?"

"Too high," I said.

She frowned, groping for words. "Not too high! What kind interest? Where we will putting? Cannot putting interest on nor' seast, bee-cause nor'seast is ba-ad place!"

It took me a little while to understand what she was trying to say, and then I saw that she was using "interest" for "entrance." In Japan, the entrance to a house is seldom put on the northeast, because that used to be the location of the "devil's gate." I told Richi-san to forget about the entrance for the time being and to take a closer look at those compound interest tables.

She did, and consulted O-jii-chan. They talked a long time.

"We must finding small carpenter," Richi-san said.

They found one, small both in stature and in the building profession. His name was Jibiki-san. He was a short, pudgy man with a Chaplinesque mustache and glib speech. He invariably wore plus-fours, and I assumed that he spent much of his time on the golf links, and attached a certain amount of desirable prosperity to his garb—until I learned that plus-fours are the uniform of building contractors in Japan. Jibiki-san was hired principally because he professed to "pu-raying same Buddha"; he was, he said, of the Nichiren sect. O-jii-chan paid him a hundred thousand yen and signed a well-documented and itemized contract, which stipulated further payments during the progress of the construction and the digging of the well. The final payment, of two hundred thousand yen, was to be made upon acceptance of the completed dwelling.

Jibiki-san hired subcontractors of every kind. Ground was broken, the well was hand-dug to sweet, soft water at a depth of sixty feet, the framework rose, the yellow tile roof went on—

according to Japanese custom—before floors or walls had been touched. Now, Richi-san informed me, I must attend the ceremony of muneage, which she called the "blessing of the bones"—that is, the framework—and I agreed to come and bring some American friends. This ritual is suggestive of our roof-raising, but has more religious overtones. All the workmen and most of the Asano kinsmen were there on the day of the ceremony; food was spread the length of two planks laid on the ground for a picnic table, and beer and sake flowed freely. Buddha was asked to bless the new house, with its ribs of two-by-fours standing stark against a lowering autumnal sky. Songs were sung, and a couple of the carpenters grew red-faced and boisterous on an incredibly small intake of sake.

Jibiki-san, squatting in his plus-fours, was the jolliest and most important of men. . . .

I DID NOT SEE THE ASANOS FOR TWO OR THREE WEEKS, AND THEN I drove by the new house on my way to Ogu-machi. The rough plastering had been done—brown mud mixed with rice straw and laid over a latticework of bamboo. That was all, and no workmen were at the house. I went on to Ogu-machi to find the Asanos so stunned by what had happened that they hardly believed it.

Jibiki-san (who said he believed in the same Buddha) had persuaded them to make the final payment of two hundred thousand yen in advance of its due date, pleading a shortage of cash for building materials, and then he had walked off the job. The floors were not finished. There were no windows, no doors, no plumbing, no lights, no heat. In addition, it developed that Jibiki-san—the only dishonest man I had met in Japan—had failed to pay the carpenters, the plasterers, and the other artisans their full due. His Tokyo office did not answer the telephone, and when I drove Richi-san and O-jii-chan there we found the place shuttered. Jibiki-san was what they called a yonige—a fly-by-night—and we learned later that he had defrauded several other home builders.

To me, a meat eater and given to anger, the meek helplessness with which the Asanos greeted this disaster was exasperating. They obtained a brief extension of the lease on the apato, because the fish-store master was "verree kindness," but the fish store had been closed, and the prospective noodle restaurant was losing prospective trade. On a cold and rainy day in mid-December, the noodle people took possession of the apato, with many an "I'm sorry," and the Asanos—riding unprotected in an open truck with their household goods and their many pets—moved into the shell of the new house. They were very careful to keep the kanariya covered and warm during this operation.

I found them there that evening—O-jii-chan, O-baa-chan, Richi-san, Masako-chan, and Shinjuku Unc' (who had helped them move)—all huddled together in a six-mat room that did not yet have its mats; newspapers had been put down over the cracks in the floor and cotton sheets hung at window and door openings in a vain attempt to keep out the wind. The family wore their heaviest clothing, had charcoal burning in two hibachi, and were drinking endless cups of hot tea. Honorable Little Grandmother was the mainstay of morale; her apple cheeks were stung with cold, but she treated the whole sad affair as a lark, and made a cheering supper of bean-curd soup, broiled fish, and steamed rice and vegetables, as if she had been accustomed to camping out all of her life. Just before it grew dark, Honorable Little Grandfather managed to rig a hundred-foot extension cord from the only building that stood on the tract—a small temporary shack—to power a single sixty-watt bulb. This small house had been built in the last week by the family owning the adjoining lot; it had electricity, but little else. I suggested that a double socket would at least enable the family to hear the radio, but Richi-san said no—they were "maybe like stealing light," and must not use much. Nothing had been unpacked but a little food; boxes and furniture were piled in the unfinished Western-sutairu living room, and the adobe-like walls of thin plaster exuded dampness. The dog, John, whined from a bed of rice straw in the open front "interest."

"John's cold," I said.

Honorable Little Grandfather's infectious laugh boomed out at this. Richi-san said, *"Not* cold, Papa-san. John maybe making children, Fazzer said. In spring. He tol' me."

"Making children? But you said John was a boy dog."

"Yiss, I'm sinking boy dog, before. But *mistake. Not* boy dog."

"That's all you need!" I said. "A litter of pups. What about Jibiki-san? Have you found him?"

"Don' find, Papa-san—we must finding him. If not finishing house, we will ask him for giving back to money."

The Asanos estimated that Jibiki-san had honestly earned about four hundred thousand yen of the seven hundred thousand they had paid him, and that it would take another two or three hundred thousand yen to finish the house—money they didn't have. I watched the cold wind flutter the flimsy cotton sheet covering the "interest," and only my hands, held over a hibachi, were warm. "Ask him, hell!" I said. "Sue him—sue him for the three hundred thousand yen, plus what he owes the workmen. And tell him to stay away from this place. If I ever see him here, I'll break his nose."

"But he *must* coming this place. If not coming here, he cannot finish to house."

"He never intended to finish this house. He's a crook—a thief. Sue him, and get another builder." I had to look up "sue" in the dictionary, because they didn't know what I was talking about. "Uttaeru! Sue him! Understand?"

The Asanos looked shocked. Richi-san said gently, "Yiss, Papa-san, we understand. We will more pu-raying to Buddha." Then, after adding new charcoal to the hibachi, she said, "Papa-san, this place will wonderful in summertime, don' you?"

THE FIRST THING TO BE SET UP IN THE UNFINISHED KOKUTERU house was the butsudan, or family altar. In the chaos of construction this took some doing. A butsudan must be placed as near the ceiling as possible; nothing may be put above it, and it is not proper for people to live over the butsudan. The Asanos considered the unfinished ceiling unworthy to be above the altar, and resorted to a custom sometimes practiced by Buddhist families who live on the ground floor of a two-story house. On the ceiling above the butsudan they thumbtacked a piece of paper inscribed with the character that means kumo, or clouds, signifying that above the clouds is infinity.

Then they made offerings of food, lighted the sacred candles, clapped their hands three times, and prayed. The prayer was still the same—"Namu-myo-ho-renge-kyo!"—chanted with rising and falling inflections for an hour at a time. The family's spiritual wants were satisfied, but their creature comforts were few. Yokohama's climate has been compared to that of Washington, D.C., and the season known as daikan, or "big cold," was coming. They could not unpack until at least one room had been finished, and they could do nothing toward finishing that one room. A few days after they moved in, they enrolled Masako-chan in the nearest school, and the three adults took civic pride in becoming members of the local P.T.A., but mainly, as the weeks went by, they hugged the hibachi or—when they were not praying—sat with their legs under the quilted covering of the kotatsu, a low, skirted table with a pot of charcoal storing heat underneath. I felt that Jibiki-san's perfidy had numbed them more than the cold, but they soon had chapped faces and hands, and they all came down with severe colds. Their many pets were much better equipped to stand the winter weather.

Still, there were little things to cheer them. The air, they said, was "verree countree"—pure and clean in contrast to that of smoky Tokyo—and sometimes an owl hooted in the pines at night. A neighbor introduced himself and graciously invited them to take nightly hot baths in his ofuro. On Christmas Day, I took them a roast turkey. Relatives came from Tokyo and were properly shocked at what had happened, but nobody had the money to hire a new contractor. Honorable Little Grandfather's slender income from the Shizukawa property was barely more than enough to buy food and charcoal.

Against their wishes, I sought out a Yokohama attorney and paid him a retainer of ten thousand yen. The Asanos thought this was a waste of money. The very mention of a lawsuit seemed to shock them, as if I had spoken of an act of violence, and I began to doubt whether they would testify against Jibiki-san, even if he could be found. New Year's came, with its customary week-long holiday in Japan, and during this period of idleness the unpaid workmen—the carpenters, the plasterers, the tinsmith and plumber and electrician —called to see how the Asanos were getting along. They were simple men, whom Jibiki-san had recruited mostly from the Totsuka area, and his dishonesty appeared to be as much of a blow to them as it had been to the Asanos. They found the family at prayer, and were invited in for Honorable Tea; and if they were not all deeply religious themselves, they were at least impressed by the Asanos' faith and touched by their plight. They consulted among themselves, and agreed that Jibiki-san had a "bad heart" and should be sued. Then Komiya-san, the plasterer, spoke for the group. He was oldest of them, and Jibiki-san owed him the most money—eighty thousand yen if he completed the plastering, which was farther along than any of the other work. He said his sons would finish that job, and that he would join in the suit against Jibiki-san for his eighty thousand yen. The other workmen were willing to do their share toward completing the kokuteru house, and the Asanos could pay them botsu-botsu, little by little.

I pointed out that Komiya-san's contract was with Jibiki-san, and warned the family to be careful. But they were moved almost to tears by Komiya-san's kindness, and quite naturally regarded the offer as an answer to their prayers—Buddha was watching over them. It was the attorney who caused further delay. Cautious, he advised against any nail's being driven until the contract with Jibiki-san had been formally terminated. This took time. It was a couple of weeks before the attorney could get this formal termination through the courts—he couldn't find Jibiki-san either. Meanwhile, the Asanos weathered the big cold as best they could.

One other serious problem remained. The family had paid Jibiki-san for certain items which the workmen could not provide—an electric motor and pressure pump for the well, lighting fixtures for the entire house, a Western-style flush toilet and washbasin, a Japanese-style bathtub, and a boira (boiler), or water heater. The workmen could not proceed very far without these and the pipe and wire necessary for their installation.

So the Asanos expressed their gratitude for the offer to help, and gave thanks to Buddha, but did not immediately authorize the workmen to go ahead. Instead, they deliberated and prayed for about a week, asking guidance. Then, one morning late in January, the kanariya greeted a reluctant sunrise with what Richi-san described to me as "oh, verree prettee songing—too muchee songing!" The kanariya, she said, was "maybe just a little like Buddha—he knows happiness news coming." Her small face was glowing with assurance, and that same happiness she said the kanariya had felt.

"And bee-sides, Papa-san," she confided, "last night I was verree good du-ream. I'm du-reaming beeg su-nakes—too many beeg su-nakes!"

"Dreaming about snakes is a good dream?" I asked warily.

"Oh, yiss, of-a course! Japanese people knows that du-ream. Su-nakes getting in small boat, somewhere going—I don' know where going. Verree good du-ream!"

"Do you ever dream about money?"

"Oh, if du-ream money, no good—maybe lost the money. But su-nakes good du-ream. That du-ream meaning we will get to money for finishing house!"

And, on the basis of dreams and the canary's song, the Asanos told the workmen to proceed.

THE WORKMEN BEGAN THEIR PRELIMINARY LABORS; BOTSU-BOTSU the carpenters put in flooring, Komiya-san's sons applied a virginal white to the mud-colored interior walls, with pink for the bathroom and mosaic tile on its floor and that of the toilet; and the tinsmith fashioned gutters under the tiled roof. Doors and windows were installed, a retaining wall was built, and a concrete sidewalk was laid—all of this much to my growing alarm. And just when the work could progress no further without the plumbing fixtures and other equipment for which there was no money, Ishikawa-san appeared.

He came unheralded out of the long past, a second or third cousin who had emigrated to Hawaii some years before the war—a stocky man who wore an aloha shirt under his business suit, and had a face the color of old, rusty iron. Richi-san barely remembered him, O-jii-chan would not have recognized him on the street, O-baa-chan recalled only that as a small boy he was excessively fond of roasted chestnuts. He was a hearty, confident man, with the easy laugh of a free conscience. He had come to discharge an old debt.

Sometime back in the thirties, O-jii-chan had lent Ishikawa-san enough money to buy a half share in a fishing boat. At present, in Hawaii, Ishikawa-san owned several fishing boats. He had just sold a seiner, and had obeyed a sudden impulse to visit his native land. Each New Year, the debt had haunted him (Japanese traditionally pay all debts by New Year's Eve), but in the first years he was away correspondence had been desultory, and then there was the war, and afterward he had not even been sure that Honorable Little Grandfather was still alive. Now the amount of the debt had to be figured. In the thirties, the yen was worth about a hundred times its deflated value today. I don't know exactly how much Ishikawa-san paid to O-jii-chan, but it was generously in excess of five hundred dollars. The Asanos were radiantly happy at this windfall, but not at all su'prised.

"See, Papa-san?" Richi-san said when she broke the good news to me. "I'm bee-fore telling you—Buddha will taking care to us!"

BY EARLY APRIL, IN THE TIME OF THE CHERRY TREES' BRIEF BEAUTY, the Asanos were well and comfortably housed behind the sixteen whispering pine trees, with a substantial stone wall on the northeast, where the devil's gate stands, and a bamboo fence and evergreen hedge on the south, east, and west. On the east side of the five-room house, which was of pleasing design, there were twenty-four feet of sliding picture windows framing the farming valley and the mountains beyond. By full spring, an astonishing array of flowers and shrubs gladdened the yard; anything O-jii-chan sticks in the ground will grow, and he does little but putter in the garden. There was a small but sunny concrete terrace, over which yellow-flowering gourd vines were rapidly climbing, and a curving walk leading from the street to what Richi-san still called the "interest." O-jii-chan had built a sizable goldfish pond at the south of the front yard, and it contained many more than "twelve people." There was bottled gas for a modern kitchen range, and O-baa-chan, the Modern U-oman, amazed everybody with Western-style cookery for which she never had a recipe. The ingenious boiler, located outside the house and fired with wood scraps and coal every afternoon, provided scalding hot water most of the time for the ofuro and the stainless steel sink; a kerosene pressure-type heater was ready to warm the twelve-mat living room when winter came. On terebi the family watched excellent Japanese programs—kabuki, samurai sword thrillers, and two famous comedians, Kingoro-san and Frankie Sakai. They also saw American imports such as Jetu Jakushonu (Jet Jackson, the Flying Commando), Junguru-no-jo-ô (Sheena, the Queen of the Jungle), Miki Runi (Mickey Rooney), an Indian horse-opera called Brave Eagle, and Pat-u-rol Highway. On Thursday evenings they had to choose between Supamanu (Superman) and Ai Rabu Rusi (I Love Lucy, starring, of course, Rusiru Boru).

Everybody was very happy. The kanariya threatened to bust a gizzard with pretty songing, the parakeets had settled their quarrels, and the other pets were content. John—there had been some talk of renaming her Joanna, but the new name was dropped—delivered five puppies on a stormy Saturday night in cherry blossom time, and then produced six more twenty-four hours later. I considered this hardly less than catastrophic.

"Eleven puppies! What in heaven's name will you do?" I asked Richi-san.

"Oh, of course we must finding homes for children. Shinjuku Aunt and Unc' will taking one puppy dog. Kyobashi Cousin 'ants one, and maybe fish-store master."

"That leaves only eight," I said gloomily.

Richi-san shrugged. "What you gonna doing, Papa-san? Maybe we must keeping. Cannot killing, bee-cause too pretty, and sorree to them. But we will praying to Buddha for puppy dogs. And now, Papa-san," she said, "we must sink about bee-ginning some kind small busy-ness, don' you?"

Outside, a gentle, radioactive rain was falling. Birds, who know nothing about atomic fallout, were twittering in the sixteen pines, and the kanariya answered from his cage. Four or five new houses were rising in the subdivision where the Asanos had pioneered after a fashion. We were still looking for Jibiki-san. And anything —even a small busy-ness—was possible under Buddha.

EIGHT

THE ABDUCTION OF ANI-CHAN

JOHN, THE SLIGHTLY MISNAMED "PUPPY DOG" OF THE ASANO
family, was the most fortunate of canines. Affection was lavished
upon her, and good food; O-jii-chan built her a substantial doghouse,
and she grew fat and sleek, and was beside herself with tail-wagging
happiness. The home on the Tokaido was not like Tokyo, where
her horizons had been the drab board fence of a small back yard
under the dripping wash; here she was free to roam, every day,
in fields and woods, and to take walks with her special protector,
Masako-chan. She sniffed warm smells that were new and exciting,
and still generations old in her consciousness: rabbits and field mice
in their secret burrows, and birds that teased her along the rows of
sweet potato vines, and wet green frogs that piped on the edges
of the rice paddies, only to splash water in her face when she came
too near. She roamed the new real estate development, and knew
what the neighbors smelled like, and what they were having for
supper. She had found her people and was happy to work for them.
At night, chained in the Asanos' yard, she challenged all comers
and dared them to violate the gate, and still she was not a noisy
dog. True, she spoke when other dogs spoke, in accordance with

the ancient Japanese saying, but she was amenable to the wishes of her people and the desires of Buddha. Once Richi-san told me:

"Bee-fore night, and night bee-fore that, Papa-san, we cannot sleeping. John too muchee wan-wan [barking]. Why, I don' know, but too muchee, was. Zo-o, last night we praying to Buddha: 'To-night, please speaking John, not so muchee wan-wan.' And, Papa-san?"

"Yes, Richi-san?"

"Last night was oh, verree quiet. Noise don' have. John don' speak, and we verree good sleeping. See, Papa-san, I'm bee-fore telling you—Buddha will always taking care to us!"

"John is a very smart dog."

"Yiss, good head, Papa-san. She will watching this place."

There was one slight letdown in the vigilance John provided, and yet she could hardly be blamed. On a night of storm and lashing rain, a sneak thief with a screwdriver and wrench stole the half-horsepower electric motor from the Asanos' well pump. This was in the back yard; John's new house was in the front yard at the time, and she could not have heard the intruder above the welter of the wind. A new motor cost O-jii-chan eighteen thousand yen—fifty dollars—at a time when he could ill afford it. He built a stout house around the new motor and the pump, nailed it tight, and moved John to the back yard.

She was a good mother to her eleven puppies, even though she seemed rather overwhelmed by such numbers and certainly was trampled under at feeding time. Shinjuku Aunt and Kyobashi Cousin and the fish-store master each took a puppy, as they had promised, and a farmer named Uchida-san, who lived half a mile away, took a fourth. The other seven were a problem. I suggested that Richi-san display them on the Tokaido Highway, with a sign to attract passing motorists.

The next time I went over to see the Asanos, she had a large card with kanji characters painted on it. I asked her to read it to me, and she said, "Ko inu no hoshii kata ni sashiagemasu."

"We should put it in English, too, because many Americans will be driving by on their way to Lake Hakone," I told her, and got out my dictionary. "Let's see, now—ko is baby, inu is dog, no is of, hoshi is need or want, kata is an oversupply, ni means for, among other things. And sashiage is to offer, or give as a present, and masu is the verb to be. So, what you're saying is something like 'An abundance of puppies for presents, there is.' Is that right?"

Richi-san looked blank. "'hat speaking, Papa-san? I'm writing this sign, maybe 'Puppy dogs 'ant somebody.'"

Perhaps she really meant "Does anybody want a puppy dog?" I will never know. But her translation of "Puppy wants somebody" was good enough, because those seven puppies—growing every day against a diminishing milk supply—were fairly panting for somebody. So I painted "Puppy Wants Somebody" on the sign, under the kanji characters, and Richi-san and Masako-chan took John's children to the highway in a large basket.

It worked. Six of the puppies found homes that day, and a couple of them were adopted by Americans. Left was the smallest, the runt of the litter, and Masako-chan, who wept as each puppy was adopted, hugged this one to her breast.

"What you gonna doing, Papa-san?" Richi-san asked. "Masako will too muchee crying if giving that puppy dog to somebody. Zo-o, we will keeping. And name Jane, Papa-san. John and Jane."

Jane thrived on what Richi-san called "special fooding," and in a couple of months the Asanos told me that she was no longer the smallest of John's children. They had seen the puppies adopted by Shinjuku Aunt and Kyobashi Cousin, who gave them good care. But now Jane was bigger and more playful than either of them. Richi-san attributed this to the fact that Jane lived in the country.

"People same, Papa-san," she told me earnestly. "Masako-chan will growing verree fast, too. Bee-cause countree air is verree cleaning, but in the Tokyo is too muchee dusting and smoking—verree ba-ad for the body. But, Papa-san?"

"Yes, Richi-san?"

"I sink Uchida-san has ba-ad heart! You knows Uchida-san—that farmer. He was taking one of John's children."

I remembered Uchida-san. Richi-san said that O-jii-chan had happened to take a walk over to Uchida-san's place and had seen the puppy dog. It was very skinny. It was almost dead, O-jii-chan reported. It never barked. Obviously Uchida-san, who had a ba-ad heart, was not giving the dog enough to eat.

"That's too bad," I said.

"Yiss, I sink so. I'm verree sorree to that puppy dog, and verree angree to Uchida-san. Zo-o, Papa-san, what you gonna doing?"

"Well, maybe you could just go to Uchida-san and ask him to give you back the puppy dog if he isn't going to feed it. Maybe you could find the dog another home."

Richi-san looked out across the little farming valley toward a pass in the pine-clad hills. Uchida-san's farm was through this gap, in a larger valley where the busy electric trains of the Tokaido Line could be heard whistling when the wind was from the east. She said, "No, Papa-san, we cannot asking for that puppy dog. Uchida-san will not giving back. Papa-san, I sink we must *stoling* that puppy dog!"

This surprised me. The Asanos always pay all their debts on or before New Year's Eve. They wouldn't even "stole" a little more electricity when their house had not yet been wired and they were borrowing sixty watts of power from a neighbor, and I am sure they had never taken anything dishonestly in their lives.

"If we stoling that puppy dog, Papa-san, will you helping to us?"

"Maybe I will," I said. "Let's walk over that way and have a look at the lay of the land."

Richi-san called Masako-chan from play, and went to get her coat. From inside the kokuteru house she asked: "What means ray of the rand—*lay* of the *land*—Papa-san?"

It was a nice afternoon for a walk. With John and Jane straining vigorously at their leashes, we went down a footpath into the little farming valley, heading eastward. Only a few hundred yards behind us was the teeming Tokaido Highway, four lanes of modern pavement at that point, roaring under the wheels of an endless stream of traffic to and from Osaka. But here was another and older world, loud only with bees in the clover or frogs croaking from the edges of the rice paddies, or birds singing in the maples and pines. The valley is divided into a score of small irregularly shaped tracts, most of them individually owned. Wheat, sweet potatoes, tomatoes, rice, and taro are grown here, and in all the fields the peasants stoop to toil the rich black volcanic earth much as their ancestors did centuries ago, wearing baggy blue trousers tied at the ankles against insects, and coolie-type conical hats made of rice straw. We went over the farther hills, through a cool forest of pine and maple and chestnut where there was almost always a sound of trickling water just off the trail, and rhododendron and azalea making spots of color in the shade. Just beyond and to the left of the pass was the buraku (hamlet) of farmhouses. They were old, with thatched roofs on which green moss had taken root, but they were gracious and substantial and charming. A bullock or two stood in nearly every open courtyard, and chickens sauntered lazily about, blowsy and content. Milk goats were tethered along the dikes between the low-lying fields—this was all rice land—and they sniffed and bleated at the dogs. When I saw Uchida-san's farmhouse, my heart was hardened toward him and I was ready to become a party to the plot. He had a big house and a big barn bursting with rice straw. Two bullocks dozed in his yard, and an alert goat lifted a quavering complaint from a small shed the instant we came into view. Uchida-san even owned a three-wheeled truck with his name on it. And there was the puppy dog, chained pitifully short in a small out-building that looked like a corncrib by Uchida-san's gate.

It was as O-jii-chan had said. The black and brown puppy, half-grown, was miserably bony from starvation. It lay on a pile of rice straw in the doorless crib, and looked at us with dull eyes. Not even the presence of two other dogs a few yards away could make it move or bark.

"Oh, ba-ad—ba-ad!" Richi-san said in a choked voice. "See, Papa-san? Don' even knowing his muzzer—John!"

"I see," I said, and the milk goat blatted at us from the adjoining shed. "And I can see we will have problems. Goats—chickens—everything to raise a rumpus when we come here to kidnap this puppy. We'd better go, now, before somebody sees us."

"What means rumpus, Papa-san?"

I told her as best I could. She said it was "verree in-ter-*est*-ing." And we went back to the kokuteru house to call O-jii-chan in from the garden, where he was sprinkling what Richi-san calls the "glory-mornings," to plot the kidnaping.

Richi-san was tremendously excited about the whole project, which to her had all the appeal of high adventure as she had seen it in spy stories and Western movies; and I will confess that I fed her excitement with elaborate preparations. I told her that yagi-san, the goat, was our greatest problem. Without doubt, we should have to silence the goat in some way before we could go inside the dog's crib.

"How, Papa-san?"

"Maybe we will have to use a commando trick. You know what garroting means? See—I twist this handkerchief around Masako-chan's neck, like this. Masako-chan is the goat. All I would have to do is tighten it."

O-jii-chan laughed heartily, but Richi-san shuddered. "Maybe hurting to goat, Papa-san. I sink so."

"A little maybe. But just for a little while. I will garrote the goat, while O-jii-chan gets the puppy dog and runs with it. When I think he has reached the pass in the hills, I will let the goat breathe again, and I will run too."

"Maybe all right, Papa-san," she said after a moment's reflection. "But first I will pu-raying to Buddha we can catching that puppy dog. We must catching. Bee-cause, if not catching, pretty soon dead."

I began to assemble equipment at the Asanos' house that might have got them in trouble with the police if the police had seen it. Sneakers, and a flashlight, and a short piece of rope, and then a half can of ether borrowed from a friend in the medical department on the pretext of cleaning some gold braid. I checked out two Marine Corps jungle-camouflage ponchos, available at the recreation office for people who were going to climb Fuji-san.

"It might be raining that night," I said, producing the ponchos. "It'll be better for us if it does rain. Besides, these are camouflaged —they're hard to see."

Richi-san sniffed at the can of ether. "Papa-san, this some kind medicine? 'Hat kind medicine?"

"Ether. *Eiteru,* you call it. Maybe I will use it to put the goat to sleep."

"Sometimes if that kind medicine taking, can waking up dead, don' you?"

"Oh, no danger unless you get too much of it. Maybe we ought to use the ether on Uchida-san—do you think so?"

"Yiss, I sink good idea." Richi-san laughed nervously. "Bee-cause goat don' doing anysing ba-ad—we must kindly to goat."

It was fun to work up the operation with all the detailed planning of taking a beachhead, and we drew a rough map of the terrain and rehearsed the role each of us would play, but I was sidetracked by official Navy duties and the project had to wait awhile. Meanwhile, Richi-san's first flush of enthusiasm, generated by anger and pity, had cooled considerably, and she began to have doubts. Her conscience was an active one. They had given the puppy dog to Uchida-san, she said, and maybe the giving was like marriage—for better or for worse. She wavered between the pangs of conscience and her desire to rescue the puppy dog, and probably she would have given up the whole scheme if a tragedy had not occurred. The following Sunday I found the household considerably upset. Jane had been missing since early morning—they didn't know how early —and Masako-chan was out making the rounds of the neighborhood, looking for her. Within minutes after I had received this intelligence, Masako-chan burst into the yard crying hysterically. At the gate stood a man holding a pitiful burden in his arms—

Jane, her four legs stiffened, her stomach terribly bloated, and her tongue lolling and dry and discolored. She had been killed by a car on the Tokaido Highway.

Masako-chan was inconsolable for the rest of the day, and both O-baa-chan and Richi-san wept while Honorable Little Grandfather tenderly placed Jane in a pine box and dug a grave for her. Then Richi-san dried her eyes and looked at me with renewed determination.

"Now we *must* stoling that puppy dog, Papa-san!" she declared. We chose the following Saturday for D day, because O-jii-chan, who had a countryman's weather wisdom, said there would be han-getsu—a half moon. I came over early, and assembled our gear in the entranceway; and then we sat late watching terebi. That evening the Japanese program was filled with the blood and thunder of a samurai sword opera, and there were several American importations. The latter included *Martin Kane, Private Detective,* in which William Gargan dashed about London wearing a trench coat as he pursued a jewel thief, and *Brave Eagle,* an Indian saga. These helped put Richi-san in the mood for Operation Puppy Dog. O-jii-chan drank more than his customary amount of sake, Masako-chan did not want to go to bed, and O-baa-chan giggled nervously behind her hand and said that if we all wound up in rogoku (jail) she would "bringing us somesing to eat."

Japanese farmers go to bed early, but we waited until after eleven o'clock before Richi-san and Honorable Little Grandfather and I started down the footpath. At the last moment, I decided not to overdo the dramatics, and left the can of ether behind.

We had two flashlights, and we went Indian file just like Brave Eagle and his warriors. There was a gray scud half hiding the moon, and wraiths of thin, scattered fog drifted low along the rice paddies like ancient ghosts. Richi-san lagged behind us, carrying one of the flashlights, and when we got to the dark woods in the pass she seemed to be having trouble with a shoe. We stopped, and she and her father held a serious, low-voiced consultation. Richi-san was talking earnestly, and although O-jii-chan laughed once or twice his mirth lacked its usual heartiness. And then there was a silence broken only by the murmur of water somewhere beside the trail.

"We'd better get going," I suggested.

Richi-san turned to me, her face a pale blur in the darkness. "Papa-san," she said emotionally, "I am verree sorree to making so muchee troubling. But I sink we cannot stoling that puppy dog, bee-cause stoling is verree bad sing. Verree sorree to him, but can't be helped. I'm changee mind. Understand, Papa-san?"

Somehow, all along, I had known it would be that way; and somehow I did not regret that we were turning back.

"But, Papa-san," Richi-san said in a brighter tone, "we will more praying to Buddha about that puppy dog, and Buddha will helping to us."

I HAPPENED TO BE AT THE ASANOS' HOUSE ONE AFTERNOON A couple of weeks later when a takushi-cab roared up the hill from the Tokaido Highway and Masako-chan jumped out of it squealing with joyous laughter and shouting for her mother to come pay the driver. She was leading the bony black and brown puppy by a strap taken from her school knapsack.

Nobody—least of all Richi-san—was at all su'prised. The dog, Masako-chan said, had suddenly appeared at her school during the noon recess. She had given it all her food and had gone hungry herself; some of the other children had shared their lunches with the puppy, and the teacher had allowed it to stay in the classroom until school was out. Then Masako-chan—with as much initiative as might have been shown by Honorable Little Grandmother, the Modern U-oman—had commandeered the takushi-cab.

"But the school must be about four miles from Uchida-san's house, and the dog would have to cross the Tokaido Highway," I said. "Do the children from Uchida-san's buraku go to that school?"

"No, no, Papa-san!" Richi-san said impatiently. "Different."

"Then how did the dog get there, I wonder."

"Was Buddha," Richi-san said simply.

She led the puppy into the yard and told John one of her children had come home. O-baa-chan brought the new dog more food and a bowl of clean water.

"And, Papa-san," Richi-san said, "we will naming this puppy dog Ani—Ani-chan. You sink prettee name?"

"Yes, a pretty name," I said. "But where did you get it?"

"Oh, you knows, Papa-san. That name same name verree famous American terebi star—Ani Oakley!"

NINE

THE LAST TIME I'LL CLIMB FUJI

AROUND THE DOYO SEASON AND THE DAY OF THE COW, A DELIGHT-
ful measure of midsummer madness seizes Japan, as if the people
were made pleasantly giddy by the heat. Thousands of lanterns
sway gently in the breeze that ruffles the surface of the lake in
Tokyo's Ueno Park; other lanterns shed their colorful glow before
hundreds of ancient shrines, and the fortunate may blunder, some
soft summer evening, into a serpentine lantern parade weaving
down dim streets to the throb of drums and the equally rhythmic
chanting of its participants. During doyo young and old dance in
the streets of towns and villages. One o-matsuri, or honorable
festival, follows another; pulsing drums and crying flutes lead to
the nearest vacant lot, where a three-tiered tower has been erected
for Bon Odori, and happy little girls, looking like dolls in their gay
kimono, dance around the middle platform, posturing and swaying
and handclapping to the lively strains of Tanko Bushi, the Coal
Miner's Song. In summertime, Richi-san once told me, the "living
is easy." It is easy because Japanese houses are made for summer,
when a whole side can be opened to the breeze. People have their
hot baths and then don yukata—summer kimono—and sit watching

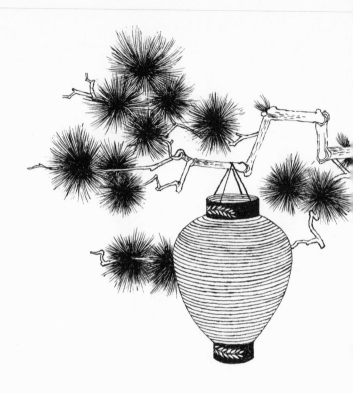

the thousands of fireflies carrying their tiny golden lanterns across the garden. Along all the little streets, flower stalls and kuda-monoya, or fruit stores, burst into symphonies of riotous colors and appetizing smells; in the fruit stores the apples are not entirely gone, and plums, peaches, and summer oranges, cherries and per-simmons, grapes and melons and pears are at their delicious best. The buses and trains are thronged with pleasure seekers on holiday. Beach resorts are crowded, and have their increase in the incidence of juvenile crime—something new in the annals of Japan. Bombs burst in the sky all over Tokyo and its suburbs to show that some little machi—once a town in its own right before it was swallowed up by the metropolis—is celebrating. Everywhere is carnival.

Summer also is the season for another sport dearly loved by the Japanese—mountain climbing.

I DON'T KNOW WHO FIRST SUGGESTED IT, BUT PROBABLY IT WAS I, who should have known better. All that first summer, when the Asano family seemed to be well established in the new kokuteru house, majestic Fuji-san towered in the southwest, more beautiful than the loveliest of ukiyoe prints. It looked invitingly near. It was a challenge.

We could have sat on the little terrace and listened to the soft sighing of the wind in the pine trees; we could have drunk beer and watched butterflies flitting in and out among the "glory-morning" vines. But Fuji-san was there in the southwest, 12,395 feet high, its summit still crowned with snow. And I said, "Let's all climb Fuji-san!"

Both Richi-san and I had climbed Fuji-san before, although the altitude got her at the 10,000-foot level and she remained at the Seventh Station while I went on to the top in company of a hardy little band of American soldiers and Marines, battle hardened in Korea. And if I did not know better than to suggest another climb, the Japanese have a very apt proverb that says, "He who has never climbed Fuji-san is a fool, but he who climbs it twice is even a greater fool."

It was Richi-san who had told me about the proverb, but now she was enthusiastic. On the previous climb, she had been the only member of the party to ride a horse to the Fifth Station, which was as far as the animal could go on the Fuji-Yoshida trail. It was the first time Richi-san had been on a horse in her life, but Geri Kupa was her favorite film star, and the Hollywood horse opera remains her favorite form of entertainment.

"I can riding horse this time, Papa-san?" she asked, eyes shining.

"Yes. You and O-baa-chan and Masako-chan will have to ride horses. O-jii-chan and I will walk. Fuji-san will separate the boys from the girls."

Any humor in that remark escaped her, and she clapped her hands at the prospect of being back in the saddle again, and proposed that we make the climb the next weekend.

"Whoa!" I said. "First, you must ask O-baa-chan and O-jii-chan if they want to go. Then ask Shinjuku Aunt and Unc', and Goto-san and Yoshii-san. And Kyobashi Cousin. And weekends are too crowded. I will get two days' leave, and we will climb Fuji-san in the middle of the week."

Honorable Little Grandmother and Honorable Little Grandfather had never climbed Fuji-san. They were highly pleased at the idea, but I know that they would have considered it impolite to refuse to go with me anywhere I suggested—it was, they thought, their duty to show me Japan. Richi-san relayed the invitation to Shinjuku Aunt and the other relatives in Tokyo.

"Papa-san," she asked me, getting out the guidebook, "what place we will bee-ginning climbing Fuji-san this time?"

I read the guide book, which said that it is unsafe to climb the mountain too early in July or after the first of September. There are six routes: Gotemba, Subashiri, Yoshida, Funatsu, Shoji, and Fuji-nomiya. We had taken the Yoshida trail before, and it was reported to be the easiest way up, but the guidebook said that the Gotemba and Subashiri trails offered the easiest descent. Coming down jars the knee cartilages at every step, which is why going downhill is hard on an old horse.

"Let's try Subashiri," I said. "But Fuji-nomiya—that's where the big Nicheren Buddhist temple is. Do you want to go there?"

"No, no, Papa-san. Some ozzer time. Bee-cause, if wearing bad clothes for climbing Fuji-san, we cannot pu-raying that place. Must put on good clothes for that kind place. And-a, Papa-san?"

"Yes, Richi-san?"

"This time, I can climbing to top—I sink so. Bee-cause, now I'm verree good helse—pu-raying to Buddha every day and living in countree making good helse."

"How about O-baa-chan and O-jii-chan?"

"Oh, yiss. Strong countree girl and countree boy. They can."

IT WAS PROBABLY EVER THUS WITH ALPINE EXPEDITIONS: THE effort expended in setting up the base camp, and in getting there, is as strenuous as the actual climb. I left the naval base at Yokosuka early on the hot and bright August morning, and found the Asanos busily boiling eggs, packing fruit, and making sandoitchi (sandwiches), feeding their numerous pets, locking up the house and arranging for a neighbor to watch it and take care of the pets in their absence. None of the Tokyo relatives could come, they said—Goto-san and Kyobashi Cousin had to work, and Shinjuku Aunt and Unc' had already climbed Fuji-san. Richi-san insisted on taking the hot bath she always took before going anywhere, and it was eleven o'clock before we finally caught a crowded local train at the Totsuka station. We stood in the aisle for the short run to Ofuna, and there we had to let two trains go by, both jam-packed with vacationists. At last we were able to find seats on an extra train, but we had to change at Kozu, and found ourselves in the sweating intimacy of a third-class coach, in a small train drawn by a small and cindery locomotive.

It was past noon, and it was half an hour before the train left. Outside, the Japanese singing insects were fiddling. Buses rolled up, filled with singing children; buses departed noisily for summer camps, and on the long platform were orderly groups of high school girls in their middy blouses and pleated blue skirts, waiting to catch still more buses. Inside, we were squeezed between mountain-bound vacationists and troops of the Japanese Ground Self-Defense Force—Japan's embryo Army—headed for mountain maneuvers in full battle pack. There was an immediate kinship, because O-jii-chan and I were similarly accoutered except for rifles or Tommy guns. We each staggered under equipment: knapsack, cartridge belt, canteen, sleeping bag, and Marine Corps poncho; I had camera gear slung over one shoulder, and both of us were burdened by fruit, sandoitchi, and other items tied up in furoshiki.

It was very hot in the train, but finally our teakettle engine emitted shrill blasts, and we fled noisily up a green mountain valley that was dotted with picturesque thatched farmhouses and laced with small, silver-thin waterfalls spilling from feathery bamboo groves. Everybody was in holiday mood. At each warning toot from the engineer there was a gay scramble to lower the windows against smoke-filled tunnels; and they had to be raised again, quickly, to combat the heat. There were numerous stops, with aisu-kurimu and bento (box lunch) vendors on the platforms. The soldiers ate endlessly and sang school songs; they were as young, and as hollow, as soldiers anywhere. The air grew cooler and was scented with a tang of mountain pine; the crowd thinned, and we came to Gotemba.

This is a resort town, sleeping in winter and thriving during the climbing season. It is still remembered, Richi-san told me, for a famous vendetta that took place centuries ago between the young Soga boys and the murderer of their father. She related the story while we had curried rice and beer.

"Was two young boys, Papa-san. Nice boys. And fazzer was killed dead—was being dead. Zo-o, young boy-sans, Jiro-san and Goro-san, was keeping after that ba-ad man killing fazzer. Sixteen yu-ears, Papa-san, keeping after that ba-ad man, but cannot finding to him. Zo-o, one day ba-ad man was climbing Fuji-san, and they catching him. Was finish."

Everything takes time in Gotemba, even today. We were there an hour and a half before we found a takushi-cab that would take us to Ichi-Gôme—First Station—where the climb begins. The driver stopped in the village of Subashiri, seven miles from Gotemba, to telephone ahead. He reserved two horses for us there, and ordered our kongozuye, or Fuji-sticks, which like everything else become progressively more expensive with the altitude. A Fuji-stick is an octagonal staff of white pine, gauged to the height of the climber.

It serves as an alpenstock on the difficult lava paths, and—when branded from bottom to top during the climb, and crowned with bunting and bells at the summit—becomes a hard-won souvenir. At Subashiri we also bought cheap wide-brimmed straw hats, guaranteed to turn a little rain, and waraji. The latter are sandals woven of rice straw. Tied outside the Japanese tabi, or split-toed sock, they give better traction and are remarkably durable. They would not fit over my Navy boots, so I had to do without them. But I wondered at the remarkable similarity of the word *waraji* to a Mexican word which also means a type of sandal—*huarache*.

At Subashiri we also acquired a gaido. It is advisable to have a guide when climbing Fuji-san, because even in midsummer, when the mountain wears rainbows around her middle, there are often hurricane winds and sleet or snow in her hair, and there is some danger. In late June that year, a student died in a snowslide near the Sixth Station (when we climbed, Americans had already scribbled their names on the simple wooden memorial marking the spot). A Yokohama candy-store owner perished two weeks later when he was separated from his party in the darkness and cold. And on the 26th of July seven hundred climbers had been forced to turn back and seek shelter from sudden hurricane winds.

Richi-san took it upon herself to question our prospective gaido, to make sure he was capable. "Papa-san," she said, "I sink verree good gaido, he will being. This yu-ear, already climbing Fuji-san forty-seven times. And can carrying forty-five kilo—maybe about one hundredy forty-five pondo up mountain. Number One gaido, I sink, Papa-san."

So we hired Tsuchiya-san. He was a sturdy, clear-eyed youth of nineteen who had been born at the foot of Fuji-san, and climbed it the first time when he was only seven. He works as a guide only during the two months of the climbing season, and his income for that period is high, by Japanese standards. When the Fuji-san weather station warns that it is no longer safe to climb the mountain—when the stationkeepers withdraw and the farewell fires are lighted in the streets at Fuji-yoshida late in August—then Tsuchiya-san seeks other employment. He weighed perhaps a hundred and twenty-five pondo, and I doubted he could carry a hundred and forty-five, as he had boasted to Richi-san. But when he seized everything we had, I didn't doubt his ability any longer. He lashed the larger pieces of equipment into a pack supported by a small A-frame; he hung the other things to his belt, and I retained my camera only by an almost physical resistance. Tsuchiya-san was a human pack horse.

I had been calling him gaido-san, but Richi-san told me there was a more honorable name for "this kind job man." It was gôriki-san, or Mr. Mountain Guide, and he was held in somewhat the same regard as the Himalayan sherpa. The gôriki does not appear to solicit climbing parties, or haggle over his fee—at least not when Americans are concerned. At one moment you do not have a gôriki for Fuji-san; the next moment a bronzed, wiry, weather-beaten man seems to have attached himself to your party, and you do have one. When you limp down the mountain some twenty hours later, he will still be with you, carrying all your portables, singing out directions for the easiest paths, keeping a wary eye on the weather, and assisting the lame and the halt. For all this, he may charge you Y1,200—less than four dollars.

We started up the mountain in a fog that dripped from the pine trees and obscured all but the immediate landscape, giving the entire scene the shadowless, floating quality of Japanese ukiyoe. O-baa-chan and Masako-chan rode double on one horse; Richi-san bestrode another, and a gaido led each. The horses cost Y2,000 apiece—by far the most expensive item of the expedition. Tsuchiya-san was far above the horse guides in station. He disdained to hang so much as a canteen on either of the animals, and during a stop for honorable tea Richi-san was moved to write a poem about him in the classical and rigid haiku style of seventeen syllables in three lines of five, seven, and five. I translated this later as best I could, and came up with:

Here the principal
Actor is the guide, who can
Shoulder all your cares.

The Subashiri trail steepened quickly after we left Ichi-Gôme,
winding through woods that smelled of pine and leaf mold. For a
time Tsuchiya-san identified rhododendrons—the Japanese call
them hakusan-shakunage—and other flowering plants for me, but
then the going grew harder, and the horses pushed ahead. This
separated me from my interpreter—Tsuchiya-san knew only a few
words of English. But it was just as well, because the mountain
was stealing my breath, and I could only grunt in answer to polite
conversation. The fog closed in even more thickly, and we could
see only the trail underfoot. Exquisite patterns of green moss
softened the volcanic rocks at the path's edge, and there were tiny
wild strawberries no bigger than a pigeon's eye. The trail was
sprinkled with a number of things, including an astonishing number of buttons which must have been popped with the effort of
climbing. Here and there were single waraji—they never seemed to
have been discarded in pairs. It was an unconscionable distance to
Ni-Gôme—Station Two—and its blessed pause for breath and honorable tea. After a time, the fog lifted, and I was soaked with
sweat, but O-jii-chan and Tsuchiya-san appeared dry enough. Finally we sighted a habitation in a bend of the trail, and there were
o-josans out front, bowing and chanting, "Irrasshanase! Dozo—
dozo!" But the horses and their guides kept going, and so did
Tsuchiya-san.

I leaned on my staff. "Ni-Gôme arimasenka?" I implored.

"Yes," said Tsuchiya-san, without breaking his short-legged
stride.

I took up the painful march again, realizing that I had asked the
question in the negative, and that Tsuchiya-san had properly answered, "Yes—this is not the Second Station." It developed that the
place was known as Station One-and-a-Half, and that it is not offi-

cially recognized. Only tourists had their Fuji-sticks branded there, and Tsuchiya-san had saved us just about fifty yen.

After that, head bent low in respect for the grade, I counted buttons in the trail. It was a good way to shut time and distance and effort out of mind, and it afforded me some consolation to find that a hundred and forty-four buttons had been popped between Station One-and-a-Half and Station Two.

The horses were already there, sweating and blowing, when O-jii-chan and I trudged up; and O-baa-chan, Richi-san, and Masako-chan, all in high spirits, were drinking honorable tea. Richi-san had fallen in love with her horse, a big, dish-faced roan. "Papa-san," she said, "someday I 'ant keeping to horse my place, every day somewhere going that horse!" She also had learned the names of the horse guides. The steed O-baa-chan and Masako-chan rode was piloted by a man named Aisaku-san, while hers was led by his young son, a student working at what the Japanese call arubeito— a spare-time job—for his food and Y200 (about fifty-six cents) a day. This inspired her to try another poem, but she didn't have time to finish it. Tsuchiya-san called "Dekakemasho!" ("Let's go!"), and her horse was brought up to one of the low tables, which was used as a mounting block.

I saw that she was mounting from the right side, and stopped her.

"Wait a minute, Richi-san! Wrong side. Cowboys and cowgirls always get on a horse from the left side—hidari. Understand?"

"Ah, so-o?" said Richi-san, and in her complete admiration for the American West she had the horse turned around. She understood, but the horse did not, and promptly proved that Japan is a land of opposites by shying and almost bucking her off. Richi-san was not alarmed; she did not even know anything unusual was happening, and through the few seconds of crisis before the horse quieted down she sat her saddle smiling.

The timber shrank and became more scattered around the Third Station, where twilight closed in and the wind picked up with an edge that searched my sweat-soaked clothing. Full darkness was flowing across the plains at the foot of the mountain, and the trail grew steeper, with switchbacks and hairpin turns. There is no Station Four, so named. The word for "four" is *shi*, which also is a word for "death," and the Japanese avoid its use just as many American skyscrapers do not admit the existence of the thirteenth floor. The lights of the Fifth Station glimmered above, looking near, but they were not. The mountain was bald and cold. In my limited Japanese, I asked O-jii-chan if his heart was all right, and he said, "Dai-jobu!" But he could hardly speak, and I noticed that Tsuchiya-san had fallen back to pace him. The altitude here was 9,000 feet, and O-jii-chan was breathing hard. We lost the horse-borne echelon of our party and fell out frequently to collapse on the trailside rocks for a moment's rest, and when we got up again, half frozen, our leg muscles had stiffened painfully. During one of our rest stops, I managed to spike some tea from the canteens with a little bourbon which I carried in miniature bottles. It did both O-jii-chan and me a world of good, and after endless time we staggered over the threshold of the Fifth Station.

Richi-san, O-baa-chan, and Masako-chan, living it up on the horses, had already been here and were gone. This surprised me, because on the previous climb up the Yoshida trail, uma-gaeshi— literally "horse sending back"—had been at the Fifth Station. On this route, Tsuchiya-san made me understand, horses could go as far as Station Seven-and-a-Half. (There used to be a Station Seven, but it was buried by an avalanche.)

Earlier arrivals had already pre-empted the single big hibachi at Station Five, and were hugging its glowing warmth. O-jii-chan and I could only sit on the edge of the tatami floor, with our feet on the cold wet earth of the entrance, and be thankful we were out of the wind. I spiked Honorable Little Grandfather's honorable tea with more honorable bourbon, and he boomed out his hearty laughter to show he was very much alive. Tsuchiya-san didn't even take off his pack.

Then rain, mixed with flinty, hard-driven sleet, began to lash the doorway. I doubted that either O-jii-chan or I could make the extra distance imposed upon us by the avalanche that had wiped out Station Seven—the new station was farther up the mountain. In a mixture of broken Japanese and frozen-handed sign language, I asked Tsuchiya-san if he could proceed to Station Seven-and-a-Half and send the horses back for us. He answered promptly, "Hai, so desu!" and sprang to his feet. Pack still on his shoulders he vanished into the driving storm. I spiked more tea for O-jii-chan, and we waited.

IT WAS A LONG TIME—AT LEAST AN HOUR AND A HALF—BEFORE Tsuchiya-san returned with the horses and his energetic "Dekake-masho!" I was lying on the tatami matting, my legs still dangling in the cold; I dozed fitfully, remembering all the time that people doomed by arctic weather always grow drowsy and pleasantly numb just before drifting into the Great White Sleep. I imagined this numbness would begin with the extremities, and found solace in the fact that one of my toes was still smarting painfully where the wet sock had rubbed it raw. Then we heard horses' hoofs sliding in the wet cinders, and Tsuchiya-san burst in. He had left his pack at Station Seven-and-a-Half, but had brought back the ponchos, and Richi-san was thoughtful enough to send me the heavy wool shirt she had borrowed at lower altitudes.

I drew the dish-faced roan. The horses of Fuji-san are big beasts, sixteen hands and more high; they look well fed, and perhaps are dedicated to their tasks on the sacred mountain. But donkeys or burros would be more suited to this employment. These two particular horses apparently had been rejoicing under the delusion that they were on their way back to the First Station, to a warmer clime and a bag of oats, their labors ended for a night unfit for man or beast. When their masters turned them around and pointed them uphill, they rebelled forcibly. O-jii-chan's mount actually plunged over the bank, which fortunately was not precipitous there, and had to be coaxed and bullied back into the trail. Mine simply stood obdurate and immovable, and when I reached for the bridle reins I discovered there weren't any. Neither was there a horn on the saddle—I had nothing to hold, and began to feel insecure, being a Texan old enough to remember cattle drives.

The proprietor of my horse fell in behind the animal and indicated, by a kindly rump rap with my Fuji-stick, that he was to proceed. Nothing happened. I leaned forward in the postage-stamp saddle and pressed with my knees—a signal that would put a cow-horse into a dead run. I dug my boot heels into his flanks. He sighed and stood. The horse master then came forward and exhibited my Fuji-stick to the horse by thrusting it before his face. This was not done in an intimidating manner; rather it seemed to be a gentle invitation for the horse to read the brands on the Fuji-stick and see for himself that they were not complete. At any rate, the gesture worked. The horse heaved another ponderous sigh, gathered himself for the effort, and started up the trail in the wake of O-jii-chan's steed. As we moved from the shelter of the station, the wind tore at us, and sleet and rain lashed our faces; and at the first and subsequent switchbacks, the horses tried to head downhill and go home. I could have felt sorry for them if I had not been freezing to death in the saddle. During the last steep half mile to Station Seven-and-a-Half, our guides had to parade the Fuji-sticks every few yards, and I tried to help by switching on my flashlight so the horse could better read the incompleted brands. We finally made it, and O-jii-chan was so stiff with cold he had to be helped from his saddle.

Station Seven-and-a-Half is a favorite resting place for climbers who hope to sleep a little and then push on to the summit to see the spectacle of Goraiko, or sunrise. The station is a sort of hostel, a long, low, barnlike structure set in a recess gouged from the mountain, its roof weighted by native rocks against the lift of the wind. Everything used or consumed there must be brought up by pack horse, or by A-frame when the horses cannot go that high. The hut is lighted by glaring white illumination from hissing carbide lamps giving off a chemical smell to mingle with the wet-blanket odor of clothing hung up to dry. The interior is built around the ubiquitous large square hole cut in the tatami floor, where eight people can huddle facing the cheery glow of the hibachi while their oshiri, or honorable backsides, freeze. Some twoscore climbers had already taken refuge there, in addition to the female contingent of our own party, when O-jii-chan and I arrived; but most of them had already turned in, and the only visible evidence of their presence was rows of futon (quilt)-covered feet arrayed beneath curtains that partitioned several alcoves from the main room. One group was a party of Fujiko, members of an organization of Fuji-san worshipers established in 1532. Fujiko members, clad in white from head to foot, climb the mountain every year, chanting "Rokkon shojo! Rokkon shojo!"—a prayer for the purification of the five senses against all evil. To them, as to many other Japanese, Fuji is quite sacred, and they worship at conveniently located Shinto shrines before and after the climb.

Also in Station Seven-and-a-Half was a middle-aged Japanese gentleman who looked incredibly dry and warm and alert. He was a jeweler from Osaka, proud of his schoolbook English and, above all, proud of the mountain. Richi-san and O-baa-chan had been talking to him, and had learned things about the mountain they had not known before. O-baa-chan, Richi-san, and Masako-chan had been in the station more than two hours, but true to the traditions of Japanese womanhood they had not eaten. They were waiting for us.

"Papa-san, we too muchee u-orried to you. Verree difficult?"

Modesty and a frozen face prevented my saying just how difficult it had been. We shivered over the hibachi, and ordered honorable tea and curried rice.

"I sink we will enjoyness this place," said Richi-san. "These people verree kindness! Same family there place we buying Fuji-sticks and-a ozzer sings. Good heart, don' you?"

Richi-san and her family go through life very humbly, expecting no more than honesty from their fellow men in overcrowded Japan. The merest act of kindness, however commercial it may be, makes their faces glow with boundless appreciation, and convinces them that people have "good heart." In Station Seven-and-a-Half, because the operators were "same family" as the people who ran the store back in Subashiri, we were getting preferential treatment—"special sarvice." More honorable tea, more curried rice, and Japanese beer.

"Papa-san, you knows was one time—many years ago—u-oman cannot climbing Fuji-san? Bee-fore eighteen hundredy seventy-two, cannot. Wada-san—" she indicated the impeccable jeweler from Osaka—"he's tol' me. He said."

Wada-san beamed. "Yiss," he said. "Fuji-san sacred."

"But now," said Richi-san, "different. Many u-oman. Was six ballet dancers climbing this year and taking pictures of dancing waltz. Was wife of American Army man—maybe colonel—climbing Fuji-san, she's put on high-heel shoes, I sink verree difficult, that climbing. And-a, Papa-san?"

"Yes, Richi-san?"

"Wada-san tol' me was man climbing Fuji-san, he has imitation leg. You sink tu-rue?"

"I don't know," I said. "Both my legs feel like imitation legs, they are so cold."

Richi-san translated this for everybody. Everybody laughed politely behind their hands, and O-jii-chan said he felt the same. Wada-san addressed me.

"Ah, so!" he said. "Now you are finding yourself on Fuji-san. Fuji-san are mountain twelve sousand, three hundredy ninety-hive feet high. What are your impression, I am interesting to know?"

"Beautiful," I said. "Big. And very difficult to climb."

"Ah, yiss. There are some old story concerning Fuji-san. It has been geological condition. Fuji-san was born of volcano maybe two sousand years ago. At same time Lake Biwa also born. Now Fuji-san are dead volcano."

"Fortunately for you and me," I said.

"Ah, yiss—ha-ha! I am climbing Fuji-san for first time. Is long dream."

"I climbed Fuji-san before," I said. "Three years ago."

"Two times?" Wada-san looked aghast. "Climbing two times? Japanese have kotowaza saying, 'If never climb Fuji-san—' "

His English faltered. I said, "Yes, I know that kotowaza. I am baka [a fool]."

Wada-san showed his gold teeth in a polite smile. "Yiss, I think so," he said. "Good night."

He bowed, wanting no more to do with me. I bowed. We went to bed.

WE WERE SUPPOSED TO ARISE AT THREE O'CLOCK, TO REACH THE summit in time for sunrise. I removed only my boots, and zipped up the sleeping bag. Bringing this along was unnecessary; the bedding at Station Seven-and-a-Half was both clean and adequate. I fell asleep listening to a variety of snores and, outside, the savage mountain winds; I woke to hear a furious onslaught of rain running over the rock-weighted roof and fluting from the eaves. It was full gray daylight. That meant we had missed the spectacle of Goraiko—but, then, there hadn't been any sunrise from Fuji-san that morning, and Tsuchiya-san had wisely allowed us to sleep.

It was five when we turned out. O-baa-chan looked like someone out of the Middle Ages. She wore her heaviest kimono coat over several sweaters, and at least two pairs of cotton quilted trousers tied at her ankles, and was a five-by-five with glowing apple cheeks. Richi-san and Masako-chan both had plastic raincoats and hats; O-jii-chan and I tented ourselves in the jungle-spotted ponchos. The horses had been sent back.

When we left the shelter of Station Seven-and-a-Half, along with a straggle of other climbers, the visibility was about thirty feet. Down on the Kanto Plain that August day, the weather was clear and hot.

O-jii-chan was obviously refreshed by several hours of sleep. O-baa-chan clearly intended taking the mountain in her short-legged, pigeon-toed stride, and of course Masako-chan was really expending no more energy than she would in a day at school—she was out front, exhorting everybody to hayaku (hurry). But Richi-san, weighing perhaps ninety-five pondo, was having difficulty getting her breath.

"Maybe not good idea, Papa-san!" she gasped. "Cannot seeing sun coming. Why we climbing to top?"

"There is no good reason," I told her, "except that we have come this far."

"What you gonna doing, Papa-san?"

"I will go on to the top. But if you want to wait—if you want to stay at the station—"

"Oh, never, Papa-san! I can."

And she started out again, up that last tortuous 2,000-odd feet, where the trail zigs and zags and sometimes the rocks are so steep that climbers have to hold on to wire cables stretched beside the path. Viewed from afar, Fuji-san is one of the loveliest sights in all the world; seen underfoot in rain and stinging sleet, it is an ugly, scarred mass of volcanic cinders that will not pack. I had to push Richi-san up some of the steeper stretches, and all of us had to rest frequently. We had honorable tea at Station Eight, and a young American told me he was leaving his Japanese girl friend there because she could climb no farther. This gave Richi-san new determination, and we set out again. Above Station Eight, the trail takes a sharp thirty-two-degree incline, and a stretch of eight cho— about a thousand yards—is called munatsuki-hatcho, or, literally, "breast striking eight cho." Here the climb strikes at the breast, indeed; it stabs both heart and lungs. We crawled crabwise along the switchbacks, hoping for a letup in the weather, but the cold rain and stinging sleet kept driving into our faces and seeking out vulnerable spots in our clothing. At one sharp turn in the trail, on the brink of a scarred ravine where snow was still piled, we rested by the memorial marker that had been erected for the student who had died in the snowslide only a few weeks before. The marker was new, but Joe Rodriguez had already been there, like Kilroy, and so had the Talbott boys, Joe and C.Y. Tsuchiya-san said "Dekakemasho!" while I was reading these onomastic evidences of American tourism, and we staggered onward and upward. Sometime around nine o'clock, I pushed Richi-san through the last torii gate, and we were at the Tenth Station—*Ju-Gôme*—and the summit. The hurricane winds literally blew us into the nearest shelter, and nobody had enough breath for even a faint cheer of triumph. But I thought I heard Tsuchiya-san sigh—not from weariness, but out of relief at getting his charges to the top. . . .

The Asanos were very disappointed. From their house beside the Tokaido Highway, Fuji-san's crest is as lovely as a white cloud towering into the summer sky. On the scene and in the sleet and rain, it was a double string of ugly frame shacks, misshapen by the wind, attractive only because they offered a chance at warmth. Hundreds of people were already here, reluctant to begin the ordeal of descent; their clothing dripped on the already shabby and dirty tatami mats, and no one could get close enough to the hibachi to dry. Our Fuji-sticks were crowned with the official climactic brands, and we had honorable tea. We ventured forth later and went to the brink of the crater—Tsuchiya-san called it "the Hole"— but we could see nothing there, and any sudden shift of the wind might easily have blown us over the edge. There seemed nothing to be gained by lingering at the apex of our achievement: we could not even get warm there, and Richi-san was still having difficulty breathing.

We moved out through the torii on the descent, while a loudspeaker blared the strains of a popular Japanese record—Kazuya Kosaka's singing of "O-tsuki no Montana," "Honorable Montana Moon." The wind shrieked its accompaniment, the rain and sleet pelted my almost-waterproof straw hat. It took us an hour to get back to the comparative comfort of Station Seven-and-a-Half, where we had curried rice again. And Richi-san, feeling better, wrote another poem in a different measure:

> Fuji wears two faces:
> From below, the slope beckoned
> Sun-warmed and gentle;
> But at Station Five the winds
> Blew sun and summer away.

Two horses, under full pack, were about to leave Station Seven-and-a-Half while we were eating. The rain stopped for a while, and Richi-san insisted they could "u-alking down and saving to money." I doubted this, because while I was moving in reverse along that "breast-striking eight cho" I had developed a gimp in my left knee and knew I was in for trouble. I held out for horses—a whole remuda of horses—a horse for everybody. The Asanos said, "Ah, so-o?" and made arrangements accordingly: the horse masters now present would unpack at Station Six, and wait there; they would also find two other sure-footed mountain beasts. This was immensely cheering. We started down, heartened by the knowledge that we would have to walk only a mile or so. The rain came up again, and the volcanic shale was treacherous underfoot—all of us suffered several prattfalls (the Japanese word is *shirimochi*) before we reached Station Six.

No horses. They told us the horses would be waiting at Station Five. We went downhill again. At one point, Honorable Little Grandfather extended his hand to assist Honorable Little Grandmother over a rocky and difficult place. They have been life partners for some fifty years, but this kindly gesture was unusual, and it sent little Masako-chan into near hysterics. She giggled that Honorable Grandparents were *avec*—a word the Japanese have borrowed from the French to apply to any couple who walk arm in arm—and even Richi-san smiled. In the old days, it was not so. The lordly male preceded his wife by several paces—and she carried all the bundles.

My left knee was killing me. I found if I threw the left foot wide, in a sort of waltz step, the pain was less. This also amused Masako-chan, who wondered audibly if I was dancing? I had Richi-san tell her yes, I was doing the Fuji Mambo, a step that would shortly sweep Japan. After an eternity, we came to Station Five, and there were no horses there either. This brought a fine glow of anger to Richi-san's face; she told Tsuchiya-san that the horse masters were men of bad hearts, and added to me, "Papa-san—all-same gang [gangsters], I sink so!" And then, becoming really angry, she resorted to the ultimate Japanese invective: "Maybe Communist!"

It is very fortunate for us, I think, that the Japanese hate Communism with a passion.

"Dekakemasho!" said Tsuchiya-san.

The sun came out brightly, and there were spectacularly beautiful double rainbows—complete from pot to pot—in the valleys below us. We looked across a mile of lava-scarred slope and saw other returning climbers using the two-mile Sunabashirii (sand-running) course for their descent. It was faster, but every now and then one of them struck a rock in his slide, and did a shirimochi that was beautiful to behold. It was clear to me that Tsuchiya-san, considering the elders and the females in his party, had wisely chosen the longer way home.

Since daylight, O-jii-chan had been casting covetous eyes on every volcanic rock beside the trail, and now that we were halfway down the sacred mountain, he began to collect them for his garden. About the same time, we came to timberline, and Richi-san was entranced with the flowering moss and other plants she had not seen the evening before because of the darkness. Masako-chan began to pick wild flowers. Our cavalcade was strung out over a quarter mile of mountain, and Tsuchiya-san began falling heir to new burdens which he assumed without complaint. He took Masako-chan afield to show her a rabbit burrow he knew—the rabbits of Fuji-san (Fuji no usagi), he said, turned white in winter. They found no arctic hares, but Masako-chan came back hugging a hat-sized porous rock, very light, and encrusted with ant eggs until it resembled a sugar loaf. This, she said, she would take to school, where all nature study is encouraged. Stimulated by this treasure, Masako-chan ranged far ahead. She came to a wooded section where the trail divided, and then it began to rain again, and she did not know which path to take. It was a real mountain thunderstorm, almost as dark as night, and split by flashes of lightning. The gloom and isolation struck terror to Masako-chan's young heart, and she had been crying, "Mama! *Mama!*" a long time before we found her. It is well known that the woods of Japan are filled with foxes, and that all foxes—in turn—are filled with evil cunning—and it took a great deal of reassuring on Richi-san's part before her little daughter was herself again.

We went through alternate rain and sunshine, and the need for horses was diminishing with every painful step. Going down was much more difficult for me than the ascent had been. Tsuchiya-san, still carrying all our effects, looked at me speculatively and asked Richi-san how much I weighed.

"Papa-san, Tsuchiya-san said if falling down anybody, he can carry. And-a he will coming back for somebody else. He said."

The idea of Tsuchiya-san's carrying my hundred and seventy-five pondo to the First Station, pickaback, and then returning for the other members of our party, was not only ludicrous, but it also spurred me on. It made me set my teeth against the pain in my left knee, and I waltzed to a point near the First Station. Then I slowed down and pretended to be examining the foliage along the trail. It took me fully ten minutes to cover the last few hundred yards.

There were no takushi-cabs, but a bus was waiting. It waited more than an hour, until six-thirty, while climbers straggled in. Just as darkness fell, we rolled into Subashiri. The party of Fujiko we had aboard—their white clothing now wet and muddied—fell out to pay homage at the Shinto shrine. The Asanos and I walked to the store where we had bought our Fuji-sticks, and where Tsuchiya-san had first attached himself to our party. He shed the pack he had carried uphill and down; he stood erect and bowed—how, I will never know. I paid him his Y1,200, and added another Y400.

"Mottainai!" said Tsuchiya-san.

This is an expressive Japanese word which means, "It is far too good for me—I do not deserve it!"

"Never," I said, feeling expansive, "has a man done so much for so many. Please take it, just do."

On that cribbed Churchillian note, we said sayonara and took a takushi-cab for Gotemba. The small train was crowded again, and we never would have found seats if it had not been for Masako-chan's clutch of ant eggs. This was loosely wrapped in a furoshiki, and stowed with other gear on the webbed baggage rack up against the warm ceiling of the coach, above two facing seats. The warmth and vibration of the train hastened the processes of nature, and in a little while the two kimono-clad Japanese ladies who sat there with their husbands became restless. After a time, the two gentlemen also began running their fingers inside their collars. Then they all moved, and I like to think that they were near their destination anyway. We occupied the seats and found that thousands of tiny larvae were dropping, ready and eager to enter the crawling stage. O-jii-chan, with much hearty laughter, deposited the ant hatchery out the window.

We were to change at Kozu. We left the small train and carried our effects up the stairs and along the overpass to the other tracks. A train was waiting, but no Japanese train ever waits a split second beyond its departure time. Richi-san, who had all the tickets, hurried aboard. I followed, carrying sleeping bag, knapsack, canteen, camera gear, a pair of Fuji-sticks, and some of the rocks O-jii-chan had collected. The warning bell rang, and Masako-chan, bringing up the rear on the platform, set up a sudden hysterical howl—Honorable Grandparents were just coming up the stairs.

The train began to move. I could barely turn around in the vestibule with all the things I carried, and was helpless. Richi-san pushed past me and stood indecisively in the doorway for a space, while the train gathered speed, and then she could no longer endure her child's screams.

She jumped, flatfooted, facing the rear of the train. I heard the back of her head strike the cement platform with a solid, sickening thump, and calculated the fall had enough force to produce concussion at the very least—perhaps even a basal skull fracture. The train was on a long curve: I saw a station official lift her to her feet and saw her put a hand to the back of her head. Then the curve shut out the scene.

I had no ticket. I could get off at the next station and perhaps find a takushi-cab to take me back to Kozu. But if the Asanos came on the next train—if, indeed, Richi-san was not in hospital—I would miss them, and they would be looking for me. The wiser course would be to ride to Fujisawa, our destination, and wait on the platform there. I went into a third-class coach and paid my fare there. The conductor came back a moment later, just as we were pulling into Chigasaki.

"Bosu-san? Bosu-san?" he asked.

"Hai, so desu," I said.

He made motions that I was to leave the train and wait for four furiendo (friends). I said, "Dai-jobu," and somehow managed to get all the gear off the train in the minute it stopped there. As I stepped on the platform, the public-address system was calling, "Captain Bos-u-wor-tu, Captain Bos-u-wor-tu!" I went to the stationmaster's office, a small shack in the middle of the long platform.

"Ah, so!" they said delightedly. "Denwa [telephone]. You stay. Prettee soon."

I told them I understood, but how badly had the lady—Asano-san —been hurt? She had bumped her head. In broken English, broken Japanese, and sign language I related the mishap. The sign language especially delighted the three Japanese in the small office. They wanted me to do it again—to stagger and fall back and pretend I was cracking my head on the cement. They poured me a cup of honorable tea, roared with laughter, gave me the only chair in the office, and asked me to do it again.

Then one of them picked up the telephone. It was summer, back down on the Kanto Plain. My clothes were drying, and moths that could never have survived on Fuji-san were fluttering round the lamps. The man on the phone was engaged in a long and animated conversation. He suddenly held out the instrument to me. I said, "Hello!" and Richi-san's voice said anxiously, "Harro! Papa-san? All right, Papa-san?"

"I am all right. But what about you? No headache?"

"Dai-jobu, Papa-san! Not headachy. We will catching next tu-rain. Time don' have—tu-rain coming—goo'-bye!"

THE RAILWAY OFFICIALS AT CHIGASAKI WERE MOST HOSPITABLE. I had to re-enact for them, again and again, how Richi-san had fallen. They poured more honorable tea, and wanted to know, very respectfully, if I really was a captain. "Honto, desuka?" they asked ("It's true, is it?"), and when I said, "Hai, so desu," they snapped to attention and saluted, and told me they were honored that I should have stopped off there. The summer warmth felt good to my ailing knee; I wanted to stroll the platform and stretch the charley-horses in my legs, but they would have none of that. I must occupy the only chair in their office, while they stood; I must drink more honorable tea. The next train finally came, and when it did I saw the heads of three Asanos sticking out the windows so I could identify their coach. But Masako-chan's head was not visible. Ma-sako-chan was being given the silent treatment.

O-jii-chan helped me wrestle the luggage aboard. Richi-san led me to a seat. I—and not she—was the person who had been put out, inconvenienced, endangered, and even injured by the mishap. She had a badly skinned elbow, and must have been bruised in other places, but there was no headache. Probably her long hair, done up in a bun at the base of her skull, had saved her.

"Don't ever do that again!" I told her when we sat down. "Don't ever jump from a moving train. It's very dangerous!"

Honorable Little Grandmother smiled and giggled behind her hand. O-jii-chan chuckled as he arranged the baggage on the rack. Only Masako-chan, who had recent tearstains on her cheeks, re-mained glum.

"I knows, Papa-san," Richi-san said. "But I knows this time some trouble would happening, bee-cause we cannot pu-raying to Buddha, these kind clothes. Bee-hore climbing Fuji-san, we needs pu-raying Buddha, Papa-san! We *must!* And-a Masako-chan too muchee crying."

"So, you jumped," I said severely. "But nothing bad would have happened if you hadn't jumped. The other people could have caught the next train. We could have waited for them at Fujisawa."

"Yiss, I know," Richi-san said. She looked at Masako-chan reproachfully, but also with a great deal of mother love. "Someday," Richi-san said, "I sink she will killing me!"

Masako-chan, in all her shyness, pretended that she understood very little English. But she understood this, or its meaning. She began to weep, and Richi-san took her in her arms, and the conductor called "Fujisawa, de gozaimasu! Fujisawa, de gozaimasu!"

The expedition had returned to base. We hobbled off the train and sought a takushi-cab. I knew, and was somehow saddened by the knowledge, that I shall never climb Fuji-san again.

TEN

MEN TO MATCH THE MOUNTAINS

"PAPA-SAN," RICHI-SAN SAID IN THAT CURIOUS WAY SHE HAS OF changing the subject abruptly, or of beginning a conversation. "Papa-san, you remember I'm bee-fore telling you, when Fazzer was young boy, he was sinking he will being sumo?"

"I remember," I said. "It was after we had been to the baseball game. And I told you I don't see how O-jii-chan could ever have been a wrestler. He is too small—he doesn't weigh enough."

We were sitting on the terrace a week or two after the climbing of Fuji-san, and the soreness had barely left my leg muscles. O-jii-chan was bustling about the garden with trowel and watering pot, working in the glory-mornings. I had known for some time that he was something of an expert in the highly stylized intricacies of Japan's Number One sport—sumo—in so far as a devoted fan can be an expert. He was always glued to the terebi when sumo wrestling was telecast; in another country he would be called an aficionado. But he weighs perhaps a hundred and thirty-five pounds. Sumo wrestlers, the idols of young and old, are of a size to match Japan's mountains—some of them weigh more than four hundred pounds.

"Yiss, small man," Richi-san agreed. "But if too muchee fooding when he was young boy, he can verree fat, and he can big. He said."

In Honorable Little Grandfather's case, I fear, this would have been wishful thinking. But if he had weighed as much as a hundred and sixty pounds in his early teens, he could have gone off to Tokyo and enrolled in a heya, which is boarding school, club, gymnasium, and training camp combined. For the next ten or a dozen years, he would have lived a highly dedicated life, monastic and feudal, playing the squire to some obese knight without armor and working his way up the ladder until he reached the class of juryo, and was entitled to have a squire of his own. And—the thought is not only curious but also rather frightening—rigorous training and what amounts almost to forced feeding probably would have put O-jii-chan into the 250- to 300-pound bracket.

This is curious, because I know of no other athletes in the world who stuff themselves deliberately to become overweight. It is frightening when one remembers that famine, not feast, has always been the usual lot of the Oriental peoples. If eating to excess can produce a race of supermen, what will happen when (and if) nine hundred million Chinese are able to fill their rice bowls and put two chickens in every pot?

Not, of course, that sumo wrestlers are actually supermen. To begin with, some of the biggest, heaviest, and most successful plainly were hypothyroid cases; to end with, many of them die before the age of forty, of overtaxed hearts or of diabetes. But in the brief ten years or so of their glory and their prime, they enjoy adulation fully equal to any ever given to a world's champion boxer, and in Japan nobody ever had a better way of life. Nor could anyone's appearance be more deceptive. The mountain of fat clothing a sumo champion is actually as solid and as hard as Fuji-san, and his hands and feet are as quick as summer lightning.

Sumo (pronounced "s'mo") literally means "horn power," and therefore is well named, because when two 350-pounders clash in Tokyo's Kokugikan arena the impact resembles the solid, shocking collision of a pair of fighting bulls. This is classical, traditional wrestling, nearly two thousand years old, heavy with ritual. A large number of matches are run off in one afternoon during the ten-day tournaments held twice yearly at Kokugikan, because the program lasts for five or six hours each day. But not all is action: there is much pomp and circumstance. Sometimes, when the elaborate preliminary ceremonies are over and two behemoths crouch facing each other in the twelve-foot ring, it is several minutes before they spring to the attack. When they do, the match seldom lasts sixty seconds.

Very probably, American spectators would not sit still for this; the Japanese eat it up. Their baseball games are fast, indeed, and very good; they are Number Two in all the world, in baseball. In 1957 the two professional major leagues in Japan played to nearly eight and a half million paying spectators, and millions of others followed the games on radio and terebi. Not that many saw sumo, with its shorter season. But sumo, native to the land, was centuries old when Abner Doubleday—as legend has it—invented baseball. O-jii-chan's boyhood ambition was not unusual; every kid in Japan dreams of growing up, and growing up big, to be a yokozuna, or grand champion.

There are forty-eight recognized holds by which a sumo wrestler can be thrown, and O-jii-chan knows them all. When the programs are on terebi, he squats comfortably on a zabuton and follows every move. The sumo wrestler's entrance to the ring is a ponderous waddle, which has become known, slangily, as the "sumo waltz." If he is a grand champion, he is preceded by the gyoji, or referee, a wizened little old man whose forefathers were all gyoji, and by two wrestlers of lesser rank, one of them carrying a samurai sword. He has a heavy white woven surcingle around his tremendous middle, and strips of white paper cut in zigzag pattern hanging from the front, nearly concealing an ornate brocaded apron fringed with gold. The rig weighs more than fifty pounds. The rope girdle symbolizes strength; the paper strips—the same kind hang from the gates of Shinto shrines—stand for purity.

The yokozuna is not yet ready to wrestle, for this is only the grand entrance—the do-hyo-iri. He squats on his heels, nimbly for his weight and girth; he bows, postures, claps his hands, and goes into what appears to be a series of setting-up exercises. Still bending, he places his feet wide apart, and raises first one and the other sidewise until they are as high as his head. Then he brings them down hard in a furious stamping that would shake the entire arena if the ring were not covered with hard-packed earth.

The crowd cheers. He is stamping evil into the earth, as legend says Tajikarao, the God of Strength, did thousands of years ago.

Following a series of such spectacles and a number of bouts between men of lesser rank, the yokozuna returns to the ring minus his elaborate paraphernalia, but wearing a heavy leather belt and a loincloth for the actual encounter. He has wrestled every day of the tournament, through a series of elimination matches. His standing and his earnings depend upon his success, although once he has reached the exalted rank of grand champion he can never be demoted.

The referee, wearing rich purple robes and carrying a fan, goes through the ritual of determining that the two contestants are worthy of meeting each other. The wrestlers crouch with their knuckles on the ground, facing each other impassively. They rise and waddle to their respective sides of the ring—the East and West camps are as well demarcated as our National and American Leagues. Their squires are waiting for them with wet towels, or with dippers of water with which to rinse their mouths. They wipe perspiration from their brows. They dip a handful of salt from a container, and turn back toward the center of the ring, nonchalantly scattering the salt on the ground and dusting their hands together. The salt, Richi-san says, is "for keeping out devils"—it is to purify the ring.

Now they squat on their heels and regard each other. The gyoji bends close, his fan poised to signal the start of the match. But it is not yet. Once more the wrestlers go back to the ringside, once more they scatter salt. The television lights are hot upon them; the

spectators murmur and shift. Vendors are crying "aisu-kurimu" and honorable tea and o-biru in the aisles; the public-address system is giving a rundown on the weights and accomplishments of the two men. They face each other again . . . and again . . . and the minutes creep. This is all part of a psychological warfare: they are attempting to get on each other's nerves, but it is unlikely that men so fat, men who sleep of nights, have any nerves. They come back to the center of the ring and drop into a crouch, knuckles on the ground again—and suddenly each drives toward the other like a football player hitting the line and hitting it hard.

Foreheads smack like battering rams against right shoulders—you can hear the collision all over the arena. Feet are well back and widely placed to form a base solid as a pyramid; arms extend and grope for the other man's belt. One wrestler suddenly straightens, bends a little backward, and makes a half sphere of his tremendous, deceptively hard and muscled belly. He has a hold on the other

man's belt; he lifts him and rolls him over the roundness of his midriff. Nothing rolls like a ball. The other man goes down, or is hoisted out of the ring, sometimes carrying the victor with him in a ponderous crash that imperils the ringside spectators, and it is all over.

If this is the last bout of the day, another sumo wrestler enters the ring to brandish and spin an unstrung bow in the symbolic closing ritual. He makes it leap and sing through the air, as skillfully as a drum major twirls his baton. Most of the audience remains to see this spectacle. The TV camera brings back, in a series of still photographs, each stage of the bout's action, and the novice viewer can understand, for the first time, what holds were used.

"Papa-san, O-jii-chan knows that kind sing Wakanohana using." (The winning hold.) "We calling yori kiri—maybe lifting on stomachy. But, Papa-san?"

"Yes, Richi-san?"

"Fazzer verree su'prised Wakanohana-san using that kind. Bee-cause, bee-fore, he was losing too many times, that same kind. This time different."

"What does the name Wakanohana mean?"

"Oh, maybe Young Frower—Flower of the Young. I sink so."

This was close enough. The newspapers said Wakanohana, last year's top sumo champion, is named "Flower of Youth."

AMONG MY AMERICAN FRIENDS WAS A COUPLE WHO RENTED A house in Kamakura and through their landlord had become ac-quainted with the people who ran a heya, or sumo camp, in Tokyo. I wanted to see the factory where they turned young boys into men mountains and made them famous. A visit was arranged, and when I asked O-jii-chan to go, he was overjoyed. He had been watching sumo wrestling for sixty years, but now he would be able to see the kind of place he would have gone to as a boy—if he had only been heavy enough to make the team.

There are many heya in Tokyo, all of them out near the Sumida River in the Ryogoku section, which is handy to the Kokugikan arena. None of them is imposing: the one we visited on a cold spring day was in a sprawling two-story unpainted frame house built around a narrow courtyard, with its own private sumo ring in a wing that abutted the street. Outside this, a crowd of sumo fans, most of them very young, had already gathered and were jostling and shoving for a vantage point at the open door. From inside, as we dismissed our takushi-cab, came thumps and grunts and hoarse shouts, interspersed with laughter. It was now ten o'clock in the morning, but O-jii-chan explained that the student wrestlers would have been up since three, working out strenuously.

"Bee-fore bu-reakfast, Papa-san," Richi-san translated. "Don' have bu-reakfast. They will eating maybe two o'clock, first time."

I didn't think I wanted to stay there four hours, because I knew the building would be cold inside. I said, "What? Will they keep wrestling until two o'clock?"

Richi-san asked her father. "Oh, no. Will stopping maybe eleven-thirty. But then students must first helping masters to taking bath, and must fixing masters' hair—like pamamento [permament], Papa-san. And then, must, cooking masters' fooding. After that they can eating."

We were conducted inside with the usual Japanese politeness. Not many Americans have visited heya, although many become ardent sumo fans while in Japan, and we were given seats of honor on the tatami floor only a few feet from the dirt-floored gymnasium. This place, it was explained while we had honorable tea, was managed by a grand champion named Matsunobori, or "Climbing (Ascent) of Pine."

Matsunobori-san has gathered around him more than forty sumo wrestlers, present and future. They ranged, on that day, from Asashio—a towering, hairy Ryukyu Islander who was already a champion and in the big money—to a big-eyed, well-framed kid of fourteen, who had just joined the Takasago Heya two days before. All the forty were in the earthen-floored gymnasium, standing close around the timbered walls and huddling for warmth, while successive teams worked out in the ring. These always consisted of knight and squire, master and pupil—a ponderous, more than mature man, and a younger, lighter aspirant to the glories of o-sumo. The tactics at first appeared brutal. The older man would open his arms and bellow a signal for attack. There was none of the posturing, and no ceremony: these could wait, and now the problem was to give all hands a good workout before eleven-thirty. The stripling would charge savagely, butt his forehead against the teacher's right shoulder, and then be flung roughly across the ring. Invariably he fell with chin tucked in and body loose and relaxed; he rolled like a cat and bounded to his feet to renew the onslaught. The principle of sumo training is attack, attack, attack; and no less important is the business of falling without being hurt, and without getting angry. Richi-san interpreted for O-jii-chan; she told me that the more the teacher loved his pupils, the more roughly he handled them. Each team worked out furiously for five or ten minutes. Then, abruptly, the teacher would turn his back just as the novice was about to start another rush, waddle over to the side of the ring, and wait for his due. The novice would make two trips with dippers of water—the first for a mouth rinse, the second to drink—and then another trip with a towel. After that, the sweating, panting boy— sometimes scratched and bleeding from minor cuts—could attend to his own wants. But nobody left the gymnasium, and everybody attentively watched the training bouts.

Except that there was a lot of horseplay around the sidelines, particularly involving a fifteen-year-old boy who was the universal favorite. He was grotesquely fat—O-jii-chan said they would have to make him more skinny, but that someday he would maybe be a champion—and he did not look exceptionally intelligent. But his pug nose was impudent, and his little eyes sparkled with pleasure, and he wore a good-humored grin that no mauling could efface. It seemed that everybody who came within reach felt that he should smash suddenly into this lad in an effort to knock him off his feet, and many of them succeeded. He had his revenge, later. Matsuno-bori-san himself, the boss of the whole enterprise, was standing unwarily about a yard from the plank wall, intently observing the team then working out in the ring, and shouting instructions to them like a coach. With no warning, the fat boy suddenly cata-pulted himself like a mountain sheep against Matsunobori's huge bulk, and slammed him into the planking with such force that the whole house rattled. It could have been that Matsunobori, near retirement, was slightly out of condition; the breath was driven from his body and his features were contorted with pain. But as soon as he could smile and speak, he commended the fat boy for his drive.

"That boy will being yokozuna, someday," Richi-san predicted. "Fazzer said. But, now, too muchee fat."

They gave the kid a real workout in the ring a little later. Asashio himself, the hairy and rugged one who doesn't have an ounce of fat on his body but who slightly resembles Primo Carnera, slapped the youngster all over the ring. The boy rolled like a ball. He got up, dripping and grinning and waddling, his breasts pendulous as an old woman's and his belly sagging over his belt, and attacked. Never did he lose that engaging grin.

Faces suddenly appeared at a window high above the street, where an enthusiastic gallery of youngsters had piled boxes to stand on, and the whole gymnasium let out an angry bellow. The faces quickly vanished.

"Was bad luck, Papa-san," Richi-san explained. "If somebody looking down on sumo from high place, verree bad luck. Somebody will being hurt!"

The training bouts proceeded. Our hosts brought more honorable tea. Now the stars of the stable were working out between themselves in vicious, smashing five-minute encounters, and the earth shook to their onslaughts. Sure enough, one of the older men— nobody except Matsunobori was over thirty—got a badly cut lip.

"See, Papa-san? I was bee-fore telling you. Zose boys in street— verree ba-ad!"

IT WAS FINALLY OVER. WE LINGERED WHILE THE GYMNASIUM cleared, and O-jii-chan chatted happily with some of the near-greats of o-sumo, and they very kindly gave him autographs and commiserated with him in his youthful disappointment. There was nothing condescending about their attitude: they were the gods and could afford to be kind. Outside in the courtyard, some of them were already having their hair dressed by their squires, and inside some were already luxuriating in the hot ofuro, getting their backs scrubbed. The rangy fourteen-year-old lad with the big eyes—the boy so fortunate as to have square shoulders and clean limbs and a hundred and sixty pondo—stood holding a wet towel, his eyes drinking in everything, his fine young body poised on eager tiptoe; and you could see that he was still in a dream he did not believe was true. There would be perhaps ten years of rigorous, monastic life ahead of him before he realized his dream. He would someday travel about the country, putting on exhibition wrestling in the tank towns, and finally, some farther day, he would advance through the juryo class—the heavyweight division—and be in the minor leagues.

And, beyond that, if he stuffed himself and put on weight, he might attain the major tournaments:

It was enough to take away the breath of any Japanese boy, and it was unthinkable that he would fail this opportunity. Watching the older novices, such as the fat boy, he turned eagerly to the tasks of cleaning up, to what he could do toward the preparation of the food.

Sumo wrestlers are famous for their prodigious appetites. It is not easy to determine whether the appetites produce champions or whether champions produce the appetites. But just as there are published records of feats of strength performed by sumo wrestlers (when Commodore Perry first came in 1853, a man named Shiranoyumi put a 140-pound sack of rice on his head, carried two sacks of the same weight in each hand, hung three more from his shoulders, and walked with the total of 1120 pounds); there also are published records of their prowess in eating. Twenty-four pounds of potatoes at one meal, eight and a half pounds of beef and six bottles of sake, more than thirty trays of noodles at a time—these are some of the demands individual sumo greats have made on the larder. Their principal dish is a fish and chicken stew called chanko-ryori, and around a heya such as Takasago, the size of the communal pot is indeed formidable. We could smell the savory fragrance of the meal before we left, and I had Richi-san ask O-jii-chan when the young boys would be able to eat. It seemed to me that fat kid had a hungry light in his eyes, and that it would take a lot of food to keep his body going.

"Oh," said Richi-san, "they will eating after ozzer people. Maybe two o'clock, Papa-san."

"And they've been up since three o'clock, wrestling, working out —with no food?"

"Oh, maybe just a little tea, Papa-san. Tea they always have."

"But I don't understand. I thought sumo wrestlers have to eat a whole lot—takusan food. If they don't eat before two in the afternoon, when is the next meal?"

She consulted O-jii-chan, who must have gone very thoroughly into the lives and customs of heya at that long-ago time when he was hoping to join one, because he knew all the answers.

"Oh, Papa-san, after that fooding at two o'clock, maybe sumo somewhere going. And-a students just keeping on eating, fooding—maybe still fooding twelve o'clock that night! Bee-cause, must beeg bodies making—fooding too muchee can't be helped!"

ELEVEN

YANKEE GHOSTS IN TOKYO BAY

I HAVE A NEWSPAPER CLIPPING TAKEN JUST THE OTHER DAY FROM the London *Sunday Express*. The story, under a Singapore dateline, was old and familiar, because it also happened in another place long ago and far away. It happened in Tokyo Bay on a black January night in 1870, when the U. S. S. *Oneida* sank in two hundred fathoms of water with the loss of ninety-seven lives. I probably would never have even heard of the *Oneida*, but the Asano family and I became curiously involved, some eighty-six years later, with an aftermath of the tragedy which is comprehensible only to the Oriental mind. Since that involvement, the story of the *Oneida* has been my favorite ghost story.

Here is the *Sunday Express* dispatch:

> SINGAPORE—A Chinese millionaire has bought a plate glass and timber mansion in the fashionable quarter of Singapore—"for 30 ghosts."
>
> He claims they are the spirits of 30 Japanese sailors who went down with their cruiser, Shiretoku Maru, when British bombers sank it in the Strait of Johore in 1945.

Forty-six-year-old Lee Ah Yong said he was plagued by strange accidents as he salvaged the ship.

The ghosts, he said, repeatedly warned him: "Find us a place to live, or we won't allow you to salvage the vessel." He added: "It's no idle threat. By work delays alone the ghosts have cost my company 50,000 pounds. When I ignored them, strange things happened."

He says, for example, that four times the ship drifted far out to sea after thick wire hawsers securing the hull to the shore were mysteriously broken.

So he bought the house and buried the skeletons of the sailors beneath the tiled floor of a richly-furnished oak-panelled bedroom.

I WOULD HAVE ASSUMED FROM THIS ARTICLE THAT THE TROUBLES OF Lee Ah Yong were ended, and that by now his company had been able to recoup its losses by the sale of scrap iron—a very valuable commodity in the Far East. He was fortunate in that the skeletons were of comparatively recent vintage, and perhaps even complete. It was not so with the *Oneida*. The pitiful collection of bones which were deposited on my desk one day in a pasteboard carton—the bones which were later to be blamed for everything from sleeplessness to miscarriages and even death—these were undeniably human, but they would not have added up to the shoulders and rib cage of one adult man. And, although the U. S. Navy command in the Far East did all it could to propitiate the ghosts of the *Oneida*, I fear it was not enough: we built no plate-glass and timber mansion to give them sanctuary. A certain salvage firm may still be having trouble with the shifting tides and drifting sands of Tokyo Bay. . . .

COMMANDER E. P. WILLIAMS, U. S. NAVY, WAS ON THE BRIDGE OF his ship that night in 1870. He had weighed anchor in Yokohama harbor while it was still light; he had successfully avoided running down any of the picturesque, lateen-sailed Japanese fishing boats

that were late in returning with their catch; he would soon nego-
tiate Uraga Straits and reach the open sea. The *Oneida*, classed as
a corvette, was a wooden steamer of six hundred and ninety-five
tons, two hundred and eleven feet long, and mounting eight six-
inch guns of Civil War type. Aboard were twenty-four officers and
a hundred and fifty-two men, homeward bound after three years
on the Asiatic Station. The muster roll of the ship's company
showed names characteristic of that era in the Yankee Navy: down-
East names from Maine and names from Boston and Gloucester,
the names of Nantucket and New Bedford whalermen, English,
Irish, Dutch, Spanish, and West Indian names, not all of them
yet enrolled on the hopeful rosters of United States citizenship.
They were of a breed that has vanished; they were stateless professional men-o'-warsmen. But men-o'-warsmen never change essentially. This crew grew its beards and did its scrimshaw souvenir
work on the Asiatic Station when the watches were long and
liberties were few; it had its occasional high moments ashore in
Hong Kong and Shanghai and Nagasaki, and on this eve of sailing
at least one duty section had returned rejoicing from a liberty in
the Yokohama yoshiwara, singing improvised verses to "My Darling
Clementine":

> In the evening, in the evening,
> When you're feeling mighty fine—
> Call a ricksha, call a ricksha,
> Tell the driver, "Number Nine!"

> When you get there, when you get there,
> You will see the Welcome sign:
> Welcome back to Yoshiwara—
> Welcome back to Number Nine!

It was a standard departure from a foreign liberty port; the more
obstreperous drunks were in the brig for safekeeping, the more
amiable had been placed in custody of their messmates. Drunk
and sober, they were bringing back to the United States the things

sailormen always brought from the Asiatic Station: oval Chinese coins with square holes in them for stringing, silk and brocade, dolls and lacquerware, sake cups and rice bowls, chopsticks and ivory miniatures and dragon rings. With these they brought their own wise and knowing memories, and their new tattoos; and the salty, traveled air they would parade in Boston and Portsmouth, Norfolk and Brooklyn.

At seven o'clock that evening, the British mail steamer *Bombay* also set forth upon Her Britannic Majesty's lawful occasions, bound from Japan to Bombay with passengers and mail. In the darkness, some fifteen miles from the Yokohama docks, the *Bombay* rammed the *Oneida,* carrying away a large section of the Yankee ship's stern.

Commander Williams, thrown to the deck by the shock of collision, piped all hands to quarters in a desperate effort to save his ship. Very probably, he never knew the identity of the ship that rammed him; hails were drowned out in the sudden shattering crash of broken beams and wrenched deck planking, and in the general confusion of unexpected shipwreck. The *Bombay,* suffering only damage to her bow, kept going at full speed. Her skipper, a Captain Eyre, testified later that he feared for the safety of his own vessel. A court of inquiry, convened at Yokohama, ruled that he had acted hastily and ill-advisedly, and that his failure to render aid constituted a breach of the 33rd section of the 63rd chapter of the Merchant Shipping Act, Amendment Act of 1862. Captain Eyre, in effect, was had up, and his certificate as a master was suspended for six calendar months.

This court action, of course, was considerably after the fact. The *Oneida* went down in the windy dark, fifteen minutes after the ramming, with little opportunity to launch lifeboats by the cumbersome methods of the time, and with too many men standing at their stations as if at drill. Of the ship's company, only two officers and fifty-seven of the crew managed the cold swim to the beach at Hashirimizu. The captain, Commander Williams, died with the ship.

In later days, Japanese living along the shore swore they had seen "blue death fires" blazing over the sea. Among a superstitious and legend-loving people, the story grew. The *Oneida* was not only a phantom ship, but she carried treasure that was worth recovering. . . .

In our own country we have many a counterpart to this legend. Any ship that was lost invariably bore a pirate's hoard; no wagon train was ever looted by Indians but that its valuables had been secreted before the tragedy. The stories of the *Oneida* took root and thrived. And the Japanese had their own version:

That the Oneida was carrying a vast fortune in gold coins, given by the Tokuzawa Shogunate in payment for an ironclad warship called the *Azuma-kan*, which had just been sold to Japan by the United States;

that the British vessel was actually a warship which had been lying in wait for the *Oneida*, and which fired four shots across the *Oneida*'s bow, then rammed her and steamed away;

that since that time, and since the development of modern salvage methods, all efforts to salvage the *Oneida*'s hulk or to recover the treasure she carried have been hindered and thwarted by the ghosts of the American sailormen. . . .

At the present writing, and despite considerable research into the archives of the Navy's Historical Section in Washington, I am still unable to separate fact from folklore. The ghosts of the *Oneida* —the Yankee ghosts of Tokyo Bay—are very real.

MY JOB, FROM SEPTEMBER, 1955, TO AUGUST, 1958, WAS THAT OF public information officer for the Navy in Japan, and I was stationed at Yokosuka, the naval base at the southern approach to Tokyo Bay. To my office one day came an unheralded delegation headed by a bronzed and fit-looking Japanese I shall call Okada-san, a man of obvious prosperity. He spoke almost no English, but had brought along an interpreter who explained that Okada-san— a former deep-sea diver, himself—was head of a salvage company that had been working on the *Oneida*.

"So," the interpreter said, "Mr. Okada has come here to ask the co-operation of the United States Navy."

I asked the callers to have coffee. This is not only a Navy tradition, but in public relations offices it is a stratagem designed to put visitors at their ease—to make them feel you are doing everything for them, when, as a matter of fact, you are wondering if you can do anything at all. The lines of responsibility are not always clearly drawn in matters of salvage in Japanese waters. They belong to the Japanese government unless the hulks lie within a certain perimeter of Yokosuka Harbor. In the latter waters, where salvage operations might interfere with ship movements or endanger the safety of persons ashore, the U. S. Navy is the authority under terms of a paper always mentioned in capital letters, the Administrative Agreement. I had never heard of the *Oneida*, but I asked her location, and breathed more freely. Her hulk lay well outside the Yokosuka perimeter. Okada-san would have to deal with the Japanese government, and would have to make his peace with thousands of Japanese fishermen who would charge that underwater blasts were scaring away all the fish and depriving them of a livelihood.

"But you do not understand," said the interpreter. "Mr. Okada has already obtained permission to do the work. But his divers cannot work because the *Oneida* is haunted by the souls of the Americans who died when she sank. This is a Navy matter."

There was a certain logic in this reasoning. Under that same Administrative Agreement, the Navy was responsible for the conduct of its personnel ashore in Japan. Was the Agreement retroactive? Did it make the Navy responsible for the conduct of its ancient ghosts?

"Mr. Okada," the interpreter was saying, "has brought a Buddhist priest from Koya-san to pray for the souls. He has paid this priest, himself. But it did not do any good, because these are Christian souls. And so"—he exhaled politely—"Mr. Okada requests the United States Navy to hold a Christian service over their bones."

"Bones?" I asked, and Mr. Okada bowed and lifted a cardboard

box to my desk. It contained fragments of human bones. They were small; they had been broken by the shifting, grinding weight of the sea. They could have been one man's, or twenty's.

"If," suggested the interpreter, "there could be a Christian burial service at the Foreign Cemetery at Yokohama . . ."

"But just how have the—er—souls been interfering with the salvage work?" I asked.

In many ways, the interpreter said. The divers heard noises and voices. The gear broke. There were various mechanical and technical difficulties. Worst of all, the divers contracted the bends even though every precaution was taken. It was plain that the souls of the *Oneida's* crew were not happy. A Christian burial service might appease them.

It seemed a small thing—a Christian thing—to do. But services over the bones of long-dead sailormen do not come under the duties of Public Information. They belong to the chaplain. And—I realized this with the fervent wish that Okada-san would never again come to haunt my office—there were other small matters. Identification— that probably belonged to the chief of Naval Personnel. And certification of death—the Bureau of Medicine and Surgery. I could see that small and pitiful heap of bones becoming entangled in a mountain of bureaucratic red tape. I sweated, and assured my visitors I would take the problem up on its proper levels. They gave me another box of relics from the *Oneida*, assured me they would submit a request in writing—along with various documents of proof —bowed, and departed.

I went to the Officers' Club and had a double Scotch.

All the problems I had foreseen arose. Among the relics of the *Oneida* left with me was a six-inch projectile, heavily encrusted with rust. I took it with me to the morning staff conference, and used it as Exhibit A in my presentation of the problem that had been dumped into my lap. Vice-Admiral Roscoe F. Good, then Commander Naval Forces Far East, looked at the shell with a jaundiced eye, and asked if it had been disarmed. Later, the deputy Chief of Staff, Captain Josephus A. Robbins, sent me a very funny letter of reprimand. I had suffered, he said, the top Navy brains of the Far East to become hazarded by my willful and careless display of explosives. I chuckled with mirth, and sent the projectile down to the Underwater Demolition people, and then stopped chuckling. They bored a hole in it (underwater) and extracted enough black powder to make quite a bang. There was, they said, an impact fuse in the nose.

The worst of it was that nobody on the staff had taken Okada-san's problem seriously, and now I began to receive the documentary proof he had promised. They were translated into English, typewritten and notarized. I give them here as they were submitted to me, changing only the names of the deponents:

It was about 94 years ago when Tokugawa, then Shogunate of Edo, or Tokyo, whose absolute power had been firm as a rock for a period of 300 years, was just beginning to open his eyes to Western Civilization, the influence of which was resulting in a rush into these small islands with a wave of overseas trade.

To lift the firm cover of a shell called the "Policy of Exclusion of Foreigners," which Tokugawa Shogunate had adopted for a long period when the Shogunate was on the decline, Tokugawa made a purchase from the United States of an ironclad ship called the Azuma-kan which was in those days one of the newest and most powerful ships afloat. Tokugawa had purchased this vessel for the purpose of obtaining power and authority over the other feudal lords of the islands. The Azuma-kan was accompanied from the United States by the Oneida, a sister ship, and was the only sea power of the Shogunate at that time. The ship was a sister ship, which crossed the ocean along with the Azuma-kan ship.

The Oneida, which was lying off the shore of Shinagawa, received the prices for the Azuma-kan, ammunitions, weapons, etc., from the Tokugawa. Upon receiving the *Koban* or gold coins as the prices, the Oneida had every piece of the gold coins judged by a Chinese, expert judge; a barge was brought alongside the back of the starboard of the Oneida, and the shipping of the coins was made under strict surveillance. At about 2 o'clock A.M., January 24th, 94 years ago, the Oneida with a crew of about 200, including the crew of the Azuma (which included women) left Yokohama Port under the screen of night. A British battleship, which was anchoring off the coast of Hashimirizu near the mouth of Tokyo Bay and waiting for the approach of the Oneida, discovered the Oneida about 5 o'clock A.M., which came to a position about 1500 meters south to the present No. 2 Coast

Battery of Tokyo Bay. The British ship suddenly fired four shots on the Oneida and attempted to stop her. As the Oneida didn't stop, the British ship dashed against the front of the starboard of the Oneida in an attempt to sink her; thus the Oneida was sunk in a few minutes. Without saving even a crew of the Oneida, the British ship sailed away. Of the crews of the Oneida, only about thirty could swim to the shore of Hashirimizu and survive the disaster. People living near the shore talked in later days about a rumor that in a gloomy dark night blue death fires were blazing over the sea where the Oneida had sunk. "It's a phantom ship!" spread among the people.

An old man, who is at present living in the shore of Hashirimizu, said that: "My grandfather was the master of a barge which had carried gold coins to the Oneida, and affirmed the shipping of the gold coins into the Oneida. My father furnished me with the above information and told me to become a diver and salvage the coins." After twenty years after the sinking of the Oneida, diving technics were originated for the first time. At this time, the old man made up his mind to become a diver. Believing firmly his father's dying wish, he set about his small-scale salvage work of the Oneida. From that time until we set about the salvage work, there were many persons who entered upon the salvage work of the Oneida, which, however, had turned out to be a failure, thus losing many precious human lives. For a period of about one and a half years, we organized an excellent salvage team consisting of the most skillful seven divers, and carried out the most large-scale salvage work with a large amount of funds (about 60,000,000 yen) at the worst spot where the depth of water is about 40 meters; the tide stretches about two miles long, and the sea is muddy. Continuous searches were made thoroughly at the bottom of the Oneida, especially at important spots. However, we failed to discover the object, and resulted in a miserable result.

It was our great pleasure, however, that we could salvage the remains of the U. S. crew that were wandering lonely in a strange country for a long period, although we failed in the salvage work on the Oneida. I do believe that the return of the remains to the United States Naval Authorities was enough to appease the soul of the dead. It was our pleasure to hear that Admiral Good expressed his gratitude over the return of the bones, and that our application is now being considered.

We are not insisting on the existence of a soul just because of a mere vacillation or sensational curiosity. We have had previous experiences, through which we insist on the existence of a soul. In the following pages I would like to report to you several main experiences selected out of those really experienced by the persons who had been engaged in the salvage work of the Oneida. We hear that the souls of the Japanese soldiers, who had died in honor in the Island of Attu in the last war, made attacks on the barracks of the United States Army who had been stationing on the island since the end of the war, and harassed the sentries; when the sentries fired on the Japanese soldiers their figures sudden vanished like a phantom. And the fact was taken up in Washington, and a plan to organize the "Japanese Soldiers Remains Collection Mission" was formed. The Mission landed on the island and discovered many corpses of the Japanese soldiers one after another when they digged up the tundra-field of the Attu. The news still remains fresh in our memory.

For a period of past one and a half years, during which period we were working on the salvage work of the Oneida, we asked the priest, Kojun Nakamura, who graduated from the Koya-san College, the head temple of the Shingon Sect which is one of the three biggest religions, for memorial services in the way of Buddhism for the remains of the dead. He brought a provisional memorial tower back to the Koya-san temple, and is at present holding memorial services for the dead. I hear that spiritualism is highly developed in your country. I do believe that they who are interested in this field will understand our experiences well. It is my sincere wish that you grasp the spirits' will, and hold a solemn memorial service for those dead, by your hands. The purpose of this report lies on the above point.

The above is composed by me, basing upon various materials.

T. Okada

OKADA-SAN'S CONCERN WAS SERIOUS AND SINCERE. HE CAME TO MY office again and again, and this was only the first of a series of affidavits that cost him time and money. He came accompanied by a stocky man named George Matsuyama, from a Yokosuka city government office. George had once been a West Coast newspaperman—in fact, he was a graduate of a California university and spoke English fully equal to my own.

"Captain," said George, "you may not believe it. But to Mr. Okada and the people working for him this is a very real problem."

I said I understood, but it was taking time to get an official service arranged. I bought George a few drinks—he could consume a formidable amount of Scotch without turning a hair, while, on the other hand, Okada-san was strictly a one-beer man—and drinking one beer always made his face turn a brick red.

I drove George and Okada-san to Yokohama, took them by the Asanos' house, and introduced them to my Japanese friends. George's superior language abilities enabled me to understand some current difficulties the Asanos were having in connection with their suit against the crooked contractor. But we left another small pasteboard carton in the Asanos' house that evening, and the next time I saw Richi-san she looked pale and drawn.

"Papa-san, what keeping that box—maybe keeping bones? I

sink so. We cannot sleeping last night and-a bee-fore night. I sink somesing verree ba-ad, that box. Papa-san please taking somewhere, don' stay our house!"

"I'm sorry," I said, wondering. "I meant to take it back to the office with me. Gomen-nasai!"

I removed the offending relics, and added them to Exhibit A in the case of Okada-san versus the Yankee ghosts. But this latest development was difficult to place on the green tablecloth of the morning staff conference, and so was the latest document sent to me by the salvage firm:

> Deposition of Eigo Harada, age 34, person responsible for salvage work of the Oneida, and collection of the remains. Deposition of Toshiko Hirada, age 26, wife of Eigo Hirada:
>
> In the following, I tell you about my experience which gave me the strongest shock while working on the salvage work of the Oneida. The incident in question took place on 19 November, 1955. My wife, Toshiko, was four months pregnant then, and it had already been three months since we started salvage work on the Oneida. The salvage work was generally going well. A good deal of the remains were already salvaged. It was about the time when rumors were here and there in circulation about the bones, from the mouth of the skipper of the Dai-ichi Kohatsu Maru. The bones already salvaged were placed in a residence of the skipper and workers, located in Kamoi, Yokosuka-shi. I feared that the existence of the bones might excite them and cause inconvenience to the operation of the salvage work, so I moved the bones to the Kamoi Kango Temple where my temporary residence was. I didn't tell even my wife about the bringing of the bones to the temple, and enshrined the bones in the room of the priest, Kojun Nakamura. It was after twelve o'clock of that night when my wife, who was sleeping beside me, suddenly appearing unusual, opened her eyes wide;

clenched her fist over her chest, convulsions over her
body trembled as if she were grasping at the air. I shouted
to her and tried to wake her by shaking, but it was of no
help. In the next moment I knew instinctively, and woke
the priest, Kojun Nakamura, who was sleeping in a next
room. I had him pray for the bones. By his praying, she
recovered to a normal condition. Then my wife told me
about her condition of that time. According to her, she
was feeling as if her whole body were being pressed down
by someone, who was tickling her whole body, although
her eyes were open and she was clearly conscious. The
first period of the salvage work was brought to a close by
30 June 1956, due to necessity of the work permit of the
Maritime Safety Board, and my first son was born, but
dead as if prearranged. (She was delivered of a dead boy
at Koizumi Hospital of Yokosuka-shi.)

Deposition of Kawabe Ichiro, age 54, of a salvage ship
of the Oneida:

Representing the crews of the Dai-ichi Kohatsu Maru,
I would like to tell you in the following pages about main
examples out of strange incidents which we learned by
experiences for the period we were engaged in the salvage
work of the Oneida.

1. During the period of the salvage work it took place
very often in the ship that we heard a voice coming from
nowhere as if someone were groaning, around 12 o'clock
to 1 o'clock of the night. One time all of the crew (13)
gathered in the ship and tried to affirm the voice by all
the crew, but we could hear no voice when we were
awake. When we went to sleep, groaning voices came
again from nowhere. After ceasing the salvage, my ship is
now anchoring in Uraga Port, but such incidents as above
never happened again.

2. Especially on the day when the straight-pipe work
(a straight pipe of 40 meters length is reached down to

the Oneida from my ship, and an investigation is carried out after exhausting earth and sand) was conducted, it occurred almost each time that some one of the crew had dreamed; was pressed down; or attacked with fever after going to sleep. And one time, such an incident took place that many faces of the Americans were displayed with the back (background) of red around the bed while being half asleep and half awake. The crew soon learned what such an incident meant, and as an incident had taken place, the crew walked over immediately to the place near the back of the starboard where a straight-pipe was, and searches were made. They were sure to discover a piece of the remains of the Oneida out of the earth and sand salvaged from the bottom of the sea.

3. Of the crew, Kobayashi was an unbeliever. One day, after finishing his work, he cleaned the place and went to bed, letting a piece of bone alone with the dusts which he gathered up. In the middle of the night, he felt as if he were pressed down by someone, and saw, while being half asleep and half awake, the Americans splashing the water and climbing up the ship. Since that time, he was always the first to handle the remains carefully.

4. During the period of the salvage work I dreamed often that among the countless jelly-fishes floating in the sea I could see many faces of the Americans. Besides me, Kobayashi, Iwazaki (he died) Yamamoto, etc., stated that they also had the same dream.

Deposition of Kotaro Fukuda, age 37, mechanical engineer.

If I remember right, the time was about the middle of December, 1955. The Kohatsu Maru was moored at a pier of the Maritime Safety Board in Uraga Port for receiving a regular inspection from the Maritime Transport Bureau. I also boarded the ship as an engineer for preparation of the regular inspection. All of the crew was off the ship on that night and I was feeling somewhat lonely and fatigued. I don't remember exactly how long I was sleeping but I was wakened by the sound of footsteps of a person walking on the upper deck. . . . I went up to the place near the entrance to the Water-side where the footsteps ceased to walk, but no figure was seen. I did hear the footsteps, which still ring in my mind. I am still wondering who the person was.

Deposition of Shoji Tokunaga, age 31, chief diver:

From my standpoint, that I was engaged in a particular work as a diver, I will report to you two strange incidents which I learned by my own experiences while conducting the salvage work at the actual spot of the Oneida, which lies at a depth of about 40 meters.

1. The incident of which I am going to tell you now is in accord with the experiences of the other six divers (though they differ somewhat according to each person). While I was working at the bottom of the sea I heard sounds like something beating a drum from the bottom of the Oneida, four or five times during the period of the whole work. The sounds lasted continuously for about 5 to 10 minutes.

2. One time, as I was deep in my work at the bottom of the sea, I heard someone calling me (though the voice or the words were not clear). I was startled with the calling voice and felt a chill and a thrill of horror. I soon came up to the surface of the sea.

3. Since the time I set about the salvage work of the Oneida, my family of four was taken ill one after another. And lastly, I suffered from a feverish complaint, which has troubled me up to date. I am still very weak after the illness. And also my wife, who is now eight months pregnant, was examined by a doctor who said that she is pregnant with an inverse child. She may be required to have a large operation.

I COULD GO ON LIKE THIS, FOR THERE WERE OTHER AFFIDAVITS—
including one by Okada-san's wife describing things that happened
when she prayed for the bones in her own home. But the tenor of
all was the same, and the plea. And, meanwhile, it had been as
I feared. There were delays. There were people in Washington
who said we should take no action in the case of the *Oneida*. The
remains, they said, could not be identified. There was danger that
descendants of the crew might, at long last, sue the government.
And throughout the entire proceedings was an unspoken but im-
plied suggestion that we were dealing with superstition, witchcraft,
and abracadabra.

This, too, would have been beside the point in so far as my own
job was concerned. Because, whatever we believed, the ghosts of
this forgotten shipwreck were very, very real to a large number
of people—some of them well educated, all of them intelligent.
The fact that they probably had been following a will-o'-the-wisp
treasure from the beginning—that they had accepted a legend as
truth—had nothing, essentially, to do with the public relations
aspects of the case. They were working at the job of salvaging the
Oneida, and they could not do their work.

Vice-Admiral Roscoe F. Good listened to both sides. He was a
fighting man—he had commanded the battleship *Washington*
during the war, when she was known as the "shootingest ship in
the Navy," and no one was ever less likely to believe in ghosts. But
he also was a diplomat, and notoriously impatient with red tape.

"Admiral," I suggested, "you are in command of all U. S. Navy
personnel in the Far East, living or dead. The ghosts of the *Oneida*
are raising hell with international relations, the People-to-People
program, and the recompression tank the Navy uses to resuscitate
Japanese deep-sea divers—we've got one in the tank most of the
time. All they want is a memorial service."

Admiral Good gave me his famous grin. "Hold the memorial
service," he said.

The chaplain made it so. If the spirits of the *Oneida* crew were

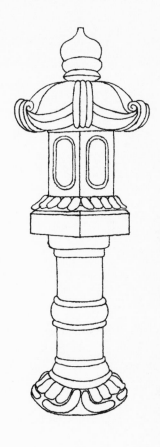

not completely happy with the rites performed at the Foreign Cemetery in Yokohama, the Japanese were. Okada-san became my good friend, and a good friend of the Asanos. He presented them a stone lantern for their garden; he came to their house with George Matsuyama, and showed me the proper way of preparing ika sashimi, or raw squid, and it was delicious.

The last I heard, he was still searching for the gold coin he thinks was put aboard Oneida. I hope he finds it.

TWELVE

LORD ASANO AND THE FORTY-SEVEN RONIN

It is impossible for us to remain under the same canopy of Heaven with the enemy of lord or father. . . . This day we shall attack Kira Kotsuke no Suke, in order to finish the deed of vengeance which was begun by our dead lord. If any honorable person should find our bodies, he is respectfully requested to open and read this document.

(Signed) Oishi Kuranosuke, retainer of
Asano Takumi no Kami, and forty-six others.

THIS WAS VENDETTA AT ITS BLOODIEST, UNDER THE SAMURAI CODE; this was the last true flowering of knighthood; and what was happening there in Old Yedo meant as much then to Japan—and means as much today—as the Alamo has ever meant to Texas. It was, in some ways, an even more useless, futile, wasteful expenditure of life. Forty-eight men were about to die—forty-seven of them as bravely, as cheerfully, and as horribly as had their master, Lord Asano. A dagger keen and clean and swift to the heart is one thing;

a 9½-inch blade plunged to the hilt in the left abdomen and then dragged slowly across the body by prescribed, unhurried ritual, severing the intestines fold by fold—that is something else. The Japanese called it seppuku, or, more vulgarly, hara-kiri.

You can still view the remarkable document quoted above, at Tokyo's Sengakuji Temple. It was the last will and testament of the famous Forty-seven, who had nothing else to leave their families or their country except the samurai tradition. The Forty-seven Ronin are buried at Sengakuji Temple, and more than two hundred and fifty years after their deaths the pilgrims still come by the thousands to burn incense on their graves and pray for their souls. There is another paper, more brief and equally remarkable: the signed receipt for "Item—One Head," and outside in the courtyard, where wooden geta of the worshipers echo hollowly along the flagstones, is a quiet, mossy-lipped pool with a circular curbing. A simple sign reads:

This Is the Well
Where the Head Was Washed

The head in question—severed, washed, delivered, and signed for—had rested uneasily on the shoulders of Lord Kira. It was the second of fifty to roll. . . .

"RICHI-SAN," I SAID, "I HAVE BEEN STUDYING ABOUT JAPAN, AND I found the story of the Forty-seven Ronin. Do you know that story?"

"Oh, of-a course, Papa-san!" she answered, her face lighting up. "Everybody knows that story. Forty-seven Ronin was verree strong men—strong heart. Was strong heart."

"I think so. But I wanted to ask you something. Their master was Lord Asano, and Asano is your family name. Do you think you are a descendant?"

"What means 'descendant,' Papa-san?"

"Do you think you are of the same family as—"

"Oh, no, Papa-san—I don' sink so. If same family, we would

being verree rich, I sink. Bee-cause was verree beeg man, and samurai."

"You would not necessarily be rich, from what I have read. Because Lord Asano's houses and lands—his fief—were confiscated by the shogunate after he died—the government took his land. Anyway, I would like to take you and your family to Sengakuji Temple, to learn more about the Forty-seven Ronin. Would you like to go?"

"Oh, yiss, Papa-san—we would muchee enjoyness that place going to! And-a, Papa-san?"

"Yes, Richi-san?"

"I will telling you verree strangee story—tu-rue story. When my was—when I was—schoolgirl, one day I was playing by small river. Down this river, coming in water, was ihai—understand ihai, Papa-san?"

I nodded. An ihai is a mortuary tablet, made of wood and kept at the family altar. It bears the name of an ancestor or a departed relative.

"That ihai, Papa-san, I don' know coming from where—maybe long way coming, bee-cause too muchee rain. But that ihai has name 'Kira-san' on it. I'm taking to Buddhist priest and showing to him. He sinking verree strangee, my family name Asano, and coming to us that ihai."

I said I thought it was strange, too, because the mortal enemy of Asano Takumi no Kami was named Kira, and neither name was common. Richi-san's find in the small river, when she was a little girl, had impressed O-jii-chan and O-baa-chan a great deal; they still remembered it, and talked about it when I took them all to Sengakuji Temple. And there, while they burned incense over the graves, I learned more about the Forty-seven Ronin. . . .

IN EIGHTEENTH-CENTURY FEUDAL JAPAN, WHEN AN INFLEXIBLE code governed men's every word and action, Lord Asano, the 36-year-old provincial ruler of the castle town of Ako, was a curious combination of powerful noble and country bumpkin, cavalier and churl. Spendthrift of courage and cautious with purse, Asano was a muscular, hot-tempered man educated in the strait-laced Confucian school. Like others of his day, he held a rebellious resentment against that education; he believed that the manly code of bushido—the way of the warrior—had given way to an effeminacy imported from China. Nobles such as he still wore two swords and walked with an exaggerated swagger, but of late a man had come to be judged by his speech, and his brocaded kimono, and the manner in which he carried his fan.

Asano was a fighting man, so vastly impatient with the elegant etiquette of the shogun's court that he refused to learn it. Now, in the cherry flowering of the 14th year of Genroku, the responsibilities for formally precise ceremony had been thrust upon him by the shogun himself. The shadowy Emperor, who lived in the ancient capital of Kyoto, had sent three high court nobles to Yedo (present-day Tokyo). The shogun, real political and military ruler of Japan, lived there in considerable splendor. Asano and another daimyo, or feudal lord, named Date, had been chosen to receive and entertain the imperial envoys. He had sent his excuses, pleading ignorance of the court etiquette, but Shogun Tsunayoshi answered that an expert courtier had been assigned to instruct both Asano and Date, and therefore they would carry out the order.

This instructor, a two-sworded Emily Post, was Lord Kira—an elegant, foppish man, older than Asano. He held higher court rank, but drew only a tenth of Asano's official salary of 53,500 koku of rice annually. Kira needed no large stipends: there were perquisites to his office—gifts, fees, and outright bribes—from every daimyo who sought the favor of the shogun. He had become more and more greedy; and his two pupils, both from the provinces and ignorant of how thoroughly Kira's palm should be greased, did not bring him presents valuable enough.

Kira insulted them both. Asano, the soldier, held his tongue on that occasion. Date returned to his own palace vowing that he would kill Kira, but an older and wiser man among his retainers hastened to the shogun's palace with a large cashbox. Asano's counselors were neither so craven nor so well informed. Toward the young Lord Date, next day, Kira abruptly changed his tune and apologized profusely for his conduct. Then he turned on Asano—a man more able to pay—with caustic criticism and sneers.

"Here, my Lord of Takumi," Kira said. "The ribbon of my stocking is undone. Be good enough to tie it for me."

Asano, fuming silently, performed this menial task. "How very clumsy you are!" Kira exclaimed. "It is plain you are a country lout, ignorant of the manners of Yedo."

There was more of this, until Asano's temper flared. He shouted "Remember!" and drew his sword.

A true samurai boasted that he never turned his back on any foe, but the craven, racketeering Kira fled. The samurai blade whistled at his back, slashing through his brocaded kimono and pinking his perfumed skin. Asano leaped in front of him, determined to finish the job, but a huge and powerful noble seized his arms from behind, and he only cut Kira's forehead.

There was hue and cry in the palace. Shogun Tsunayoshi heard the news as he soaked in his own perfumed morning bath. There may have been more than one reason why he took Kira's side; at any rate, he purpled with rage. Without inquiring into the causes of the quarrel, he ordered Asano stripped of his ceremonial robes and delivered into the custody of Lord Tamura, whose residence was only a short distance from the moated palace where the Emperor lives today. And he had Asano transported there in a wicker palanquin, roped like a beast in a cage. . . .

NOW THE STAGE WAS SET FOR THE REAL-LIFE ENACTMENT OF ONE of those slow, tragic, classical dramas called kabuki, still dear to the hearts of the Japanese. Asano knew what he could expect. He might be exonerated and set free. He could be treated like a common criminal and put to death by strangulation. Or—and this was most likely—the shogun, in gracious consideration of Asano's rank, might allow him the privilege of performing hara-kiri—literally "belly cutting open."

From earliest childhood, Lord Asano and all the samurai of his day had been prepared for that sort of death, even down to the most minute details as to how the ceremony should be accomplished.

Swift couriers left Yedo at eleven o'clock that morning, soon after the palace brawl, with word for Asano's beautiful wife and his retainers in the castle town of Ako. The distance was four hundred miles. The dispatch riders covered it in four and a half days. Long before that time, Asano was dead, and other couriers were on their way bearing his last words—a tanka-style ode, written in the traditionally classic 31 syllables. It has been translated:

> Frailer far than the tender flowers
> That are soon scattered by the wind,
> Must I now bid a last farewell
> And leave the genial spring behind?

It would be difficult to say just when the rite of seppuku, or hara-kiri, was first established in Japan; it would be even more difficult to determine how and when it became an art form. Originally, perhaps, it was a mode of suicide for samurai who had no choice left them but to die. In even older days, a retainer disemboweled himself after his master's death, so as to serve him in the other world. Too many good fighting men expended themselves in this way, and there were imperial edicts forbidding the practice. It then became the custom to condemn—or rather to permit—nobles and samurai adjudged guilty of a crime to kill themselves in this manner. A more painful or horrible way of death can hardly be imagined. But the bushido code embraced the difficult ways; it scorned anything painless or easy.

Asano had been taken to Tamura's palace at the Hour of the Monkey—between three and five in the afternoon. In the tradition of condemned men the world over (is it caused by nervousness?) he ate a hearty meal—a bowl of soup and five dishes—then drank two cups of warm water. At the Hour of the Cock (between five and seven) he was ready.

A white curtain was hung in the garden. Two straw mats were arranged at right angles, in the shape of a hammer; a white cloth and a rug were spread. The rug was red—it would not show the blood. The ceremonial enclosure, by regulation, was thirty-six feet square, and matting was placed leading to it, so that Lord Asano would not suffer loss of face by tripping or losing a sandal. There were two entrances. The door to the south was called shugiyomon— the door of the practice of virtue—and that to the north, umbanmon —unaccountably, the door of the warm basin. Candles burned in saucers placed on stands of bamboo four feet high and wrapped in white silk.

The principal entered by the gate of the warm basin; the witnesses and the all-important second entered, at the same time, by the door of the practice of virtue. All these attendants, dressed in ceremonial robes of hemp, had already checked the arrangements. Tea and refreshments had been put before them by Lord Tamura, but according to custom they had declined to eat or drink until their official duties had been performed. Retainers of Tamura had gone to Asano's room to inform him that he should don the ceremonial white robes of death. The official witnesses took their places; Asano was flanked by six attendants and preceded by one man of the fourth rank, who wore a dirk, but no sword. This group was followed by one yonin—a councilor of the second class.

The sentence was read. Asano was permitted to leave the garden and again change clothes. He came back to the ceremonial mat and knelt in the Oriental fashion and sat on his feet. Carefully he tucked the wide sleeves of his kimono under his knees, so that he would be sure to fall forward in death—to fall backward would be a disgrace.

The assistant second brought a dirk on a tray and placed it before Asano. All the elaborate ceremony had been meticulously observed.

Asano reached for the dagger with a steady hand. He turned the keen point toward his body. The official witness sat rigid; the candles flickered in a little stirring of air. There was a rustle of silk, and the 9½-inch blade was buried in Asano's left abdomen.

He did not change facial expression; nothing in his limbs showed his agony. He thanked Lord Tamura for his consideration—and all during his polite, formalized speech, the blade was being drawn from left to right across his lower belly.

Then, at a time prescribed by ritual, and with a skill and strength that were his pride, the first second struck from behind with a heavy sword. The blow severed Asano's head at the base of his neck.

A man's best friend was usually counted upon to do this job. To bungle it—to strike too low or too high—was the nadir in court etiquette; and to use the principal's own sword was considered eminently fitting. Samurai called upon to perform this office vied with one another in developing it into a fine art. It was held to have been particularly well performed when the head was severed with such nicety that it hung only by a piece of skin, and yet did not fall to the rug. In the latter case, a tray was placed beneath and the final skin was cut by a second's dirk. Then the junior second dropped to his knees very respectfully and lifted the head by its topknot of hair to exhibit both the left and right profiles to the witnesses for proper identification. It may be suggested here that any wrong identity would have been discovered a trifle late at this stage. In the case of baldheaded men, with no handy topknot, it was quite proper to lift the head upon a dirk thrust conveniently into the left ear.

IN SUCH A MANNER, OFFICIALLY AND CEREMONIOUSLY, ASANO Takumi no Kami lost his head. On the same day, his two houses in Yedo were confiscated by the shogunate, and his younger brother, Daigaku—who could in no way be blamed for what had happened—was imprisoned. The fief of Ako, Lord Asano's holding under the feudal system, was liquidated. This threw three hundred samurai out of work. They had been serving the House of Asano, and now they were liquidated too. They automatically became ronin—literally, "wave men," washed hither and yon by the tides of fortune.

On the morning after the first couriers had arrived at the castle town of Ako, the second couriers came with the news of Asano's death and the confiscation of his estate. The three hundred samurai held immediate consultation, and the council went on for two days, with the masterless retainers divided into two camps. The group led by Oishi Kuranosuke agreed that the sentence passed upon Lord Asano was fair and just, in so far as his death was concerned, but declared that the shogun had committed a wrong in confiscating the fief while he allowed Lord Kira to go unpunished. Oishi-san said the fief should have been continued under Asano's younger brother, and vowed he would die in support of that stand. The other group was for complete submission to the shogun's decrees.

Oishi-san was shrewd in the knowledge of human nature. In taking his stand he was weeding out the weaker members of the clan. There were more than a hundred men on his side; they were to be further reduced by more severe tests of their loyalty and courage. An appeal to the shogun failed, and now Oishi-san called for men who would be willing to die defending the castle against the shogun's troops—men who would perish, he said, "with their heads pillowed on the fallen stones."

Sixty-one signed this oath to fight to the death, and then Oishi-san turned crafty. It would be futile, he told them, to die in such suicidal fashion without either having preserved the castle or avenged themselves upon Lord Kira. He fought for time, and urged patience until the fief was actually confiscated. This took place a few months later. The castle of Ako was turned over to another daimyo. Asano's pretty widow shaved her head and became a nun. The direct family line had been extinguished. Now Oishi-san tested the mettle of his sixty-one ronin by returning to them their signed oaths, freeing them from all promises, and advising them to take up lives as tradesmen or craftsmen. The less stout of heart wavered and took him at his word. Forty-six—including Oishi-san's own fifteen-year-old son—returned to him singly, or in twos and threes, to insist that he lead them in revenge.

These were the men Oishi-san wanted, but patience and cautious planning still were paramount. Lord Kira was having Asano's followers spied on, day and night. Oishi-san ordered the ronin to scatter and give up all semblance of the samurai's life. They sold their armor—and later, in secret home workshops, were to make the crude chain mail, the helmets and shoulder guards that are still on pitiful display at Sengakuji shrine. Oishi-san himself divorced the wife of his bosom, whom he dearly loved, and took up fast and loose living in the pleasure palaces of Kyoto. Kira's spies watched him there for months, and returned to their master with scornful laughter. Oishi-san, they said, had even taken a pretty young joro (prostitute) for his mistress; he could be found tippling sake every night in the tearooms. His young son, they added, had elected to remain with the dissolute father.

All of this was true. One Satsuma man, destined to play a strange part in the ultimate tragedy, came upon Oishi-san swinishly drunk and asleep in a gutter in the gay Gion quarter, surrounded by a jeering crowd. The Satsuma man, revering the samurai ideals, saw nothing humorous in the spectacle.

"Why, is this not Kuranosuke Oishi?" he cried. "The samurai who failed to avenge his dead lord, but turned instead to women and wine?" Then he walked on Oishi-san's face and spat contemptuously upon him. "You are not worthy of the name samurai!"

Lord Kira heard about that, and breathed more freely. What he did not know was that the other forty-six ronin had come, by twos and threes, to Yedo. They were all in the city now; some of them, disguised as workmen and peddlers, had actually been inside his palace. They were able to send Oishi-san a plan of the rooms and valuable intelligence concerning the strength and disposition of the palace guard.

The waiting was almost ended.

Oishi-san secretly left Kyoto and surreptitiously joined his men in Yedo to perfect final plans. There came a night in December when a heavy snow was falling and all honest and peaceful men were asleep. The forty-seven ronin assembled and divided into two groups. Oishi-san commanded one party, which was to attack the front gate; his son Chikara, now sixteen, led the group to assault the postern. The forty-seven had a farewell feast, and Oishi-san warned them against needless slaughter: the one man they wanted was Lord Kira. Then they moved out. Four men, using rope ladders, gained access over the walls to the courtyard and surprised the guard there, but were unable to find the keys to the gate. There was now no time to lose. The alarm was spreading throughout the grounds and in the palace itself. The ronin under Oishi-san battered open the front gate, and Oishi-san beat the battle drum as he led his men inside. There, he sent a strangely courteous message to Kira's neighbors, all men of influence and power:

"We, the ronin once serving Asano Takumi no Kami, this night will break into the palace of Kira Kotsuke no Suke to avenge our master. We are neither robbers nor ruffians. No harm will befall the adjacent houses, so please set your minds at ease."

This was all according to the honorable code and the neighbors of Lord Kira received it with understanding. It was none of their affair, and, besides, none of them was fond of Kira. They remained abed.

Ten of Kira's samurai, swords drawn, rushed into the main chamber of the palace to defend their master. The ronin broke down the door and attacked them, and Chikara's party, with beautiful timing, stormed in the back way. There was a great slashing of draperies and screens. Kira's retainers fought bravely, but died, and none of the ronin was killed. The rest of the palace guard joined the fight, which spilled over into the inner courtyard, but they were no match for the inspired wave men. Oishi-san sat on a camp stool and directed his combined forces by waving a tasseled baton. Kira attempted to send a message to his father-in-law, asking help, but archers posted on the roof made pincushions of his couriers. Oishi-san kept shouting, "Our only enemy is Lord Kira! Let someone go inside and bring him out, dead or alive!"

Kira, his wife and some women servants, had taken shelter in a closet off the palatial veranda, with three samurai swordmen guarding the door. For a while this trio gave such fierce and expert resistance that the ronin were thrown back. Then Oishi-san upbraided his men in the manner of much later sergeants, reminding them that they could not live forever, and turned to his son, the sixteen-year-old Chikara.

"Here, boy!" he shouted. "Engage these swordsmen. If they are too strong for you, then die fighting them!"

The boy Chikara seized a spear and gave battle to one of the samurai, a man named Waku. The stronger, older man forced Chikara to give ground until they were fighting in the garden, where Chikara tripped and fell in a lily pond. Waku became too sure of himself at that point, and Chikara speared him in the leg. Waku fell, hamstrung, and the boy climbed dripping out of the icy water and killed him.

Meanwhile, the other two swordsmen had been slain, but the closet was found empty. Oishi-san divided the ronin into several searching parties; they found and felt Kira's bed, and reported that it was still warm—he could not be far away. Finally a sword cut down a picture hanging on the wall, and revealed an opening that led into a secret courtyard. The ronin rushed into this place, killed two samurai, and wounded a third man who was dressed in white. When they dragged the latter into the light of a lantern, they saw a scar on his forehead—a scar from the wound inflicted by Lord Asano. The search was ended. This was Lord Kira, scared out of his nobility, reduced to a trembling, groveling imitation of a man. Still, he was a daimyo—an honored name—and was entitled to die honorably. Oishi-san gave him that choice, begging him to commit hara-kiri in the honorable fashion.

Kira gave no coherent answer, but cowered in abject terror, and Oishi-san suffered from the shame a brave man feels when he sees cowardice. It was useless to plead any more. He lifted his samurai sword, half in hate, half in pity. The blade flashed in a whistling two-handed sweep, and Lord Kira's head rolled on the flagstones.

They put it carefully into a bucket, extinguished all the lights and fires in the conquered palace, and marched out the front gate in a body. It was now almost six in the morning and a gray, snow-flurried dawn was breaking over Japan. The death of Lord Asano had been avenged against heavy odds and without the loss of a single man. But there was still much to be done, and each of the forty-seven ronin knew that his own life was forfeit.

Daylight broke full as they trooped through the city's streets on their way to the temple at Sengakuji, and crowds of people came out to bow in silent homage as they passed. The first few miles of their march were tense with the expectancy of an attack from retainers of Kira's father-in-law, but when they approached the palace of Matsudaira Aki no Kami—one of the chief daimyos of Japan—he sent word that his own samurai stood ready to defend the ronin. No attack came. They were taken into the palace of the Prince of Sendai and given wine and rice, because, the Prince said, "You must be hungry and tired after your night's work." Finally, they reached the shrine where Lord Asano was buried.

It was there that they washed Kira's head in the well and placed it as an offering before Asano's tomb. With the priests of the temple assisting, they each burned incense, one at a time, on the grave. Then followed a ceremony strange to Western thinking, but perfectly logical and proper in a time and place in which ancestor worship had been developed to the stature of a full religion. They made a formal address to the ghost of Lord Asano. This was both spoken and written, with the manuscript being laid upon the tomb. It was preserved, and Mitford's translation of it follows:

> The fifteenth year of Genroku (1703 A.D.), the twelfth month, the fifteenth day. —We have come this day to do homage here: forty-seven men in all, from Oishi Kurano-suke down to the foot soldier Terasaka Kichiyemon—all cheerfully about to lay down our lives on your behalf. We reverently announce this to the honored spirit of our dead master. On the fourteenth day of the third month of last year, our honored master was pleased to attack Kira Kotsuke no Suke, for what reason we know not. Our honored master put an end to his own life; but Kira Kotsuke no Suke lived. Although we fear that after the decree issued by the Government, this plot of ours will be displeas-

ing to our honored master, still we, who have eaten of
your food, could not without blushing repeat the verse,
"Thou shalt not live under the same heaven, nor tread
the same earth with the enemy of thy father or lord,"
nor could we have dared leave hell (Hades) and present
ourselves before you in Paradise, unless we had carried
out the vengeance which you began. Verily, we have
trodden the snow for one day, nay, for two days, and have
tasted food but once. The old and decrepit, the sick and
ailing, have come forth gladly to lay down their lives.
Men might laugh at us, as at grasshoppers trusting in the
strength of their arms, and thus shame our honored lord;
but we could not halt in our deed of vengeance. Having
thus taken counsel together last night, we have escorted
my Lord Kotsuke no Suke hither to your tomb. This dirk,
by which our honored lord set great store last year, and
entrusted to our care, we now bring back. If your noble
spirit be now present before this tomb, we pray you, as a
sign, to take the dirk, and, striking the head of your
enemy with it a second time, to dispel your hatred forever. This is the respectful statement of forty-seven men.

The dirk was placed on the tomb along with the head and the
manuscript of the address. The chroniclers do not tell us whether
or not there was a sign from Lord Asano's spirit, but it appears that
the head escaped further injury. It was delivered later to Kira's
kinsmen by the priests of the temple; and the forty-seven ronin—
although acclaimed throughout the land as heroes—were delivered
into the custody of four separate daimyos to await trial. Sentence
was a foregone conclusion. It said they had neither respected the
dignity of the city of Yedo nor feared the government of the shogun. It added that they had violently broken into the home of their
enemy and had murdered him. It ordered them to perform hara-
kiri.

They died on the day of their judgment, in four groups, at the palaces of the daimyos charged with their custody. Even to Chikara, the sixteen-year-old, they died as bravely and as honorably as they had fought. Being heroes, they were buried alongside Lord Asano at Sengakuji. Like the heroes of the Alamo, more than a century later, they were magnificent in defeat and more glorious in death than they would have been in survival. The spirit of bushido—the way of the warrior—underwent a revival in Japan.

Throngs came to Sengakuji Temple to pray for the ronin, to pay homage and burn incense, and one of the worshipers was the Satsuma man who had reviled Oishi-san in Kyoto. He prostrated himself before Oishi's grave and made a little speech to Oishi's ghost. He said that when he saw Oishi drunk in the street and called him faithless and spat upon him, he did not know that Oishi was secretly plotting the revenge of a true samurai. Now, he said, he had come to ask pardon and offer atonement.

Then he drew his dirk and performed hara-kiri on the spot, where Oishi's ghost could watch. The chief priest of the temple rewarded this sacrifice by burying him alongside the heroic forty-seven. With Asano's tomb, that makes forty-nine in all at Sengakuji.

THIRTEEN

THE PLUM AND THE TOOTHACHE TREE

DURING THEIR FIRST YEAR IN THE NEW KOKUTERU HOUSE, THE Asanos were almost childishly happy, despite the fact that they suffered from what Richi-san called "too muchee troubling." Every day in spring and summer they discovered some new delight in country living, some small loveliness in their garden or in the nearby fields and woods. It was everywhere a season of growth and change: they were finishing their own home botsu-botsu (little by little), and down the street from the corner where they had pioneered a score of other small, neat houses sprang up, each with pleasingly different design and varying color of tile roof, each with its little garden. The flat-topped hill overlooking the Tokaido Highway had been included in Tokyo's vast "Green Belt" system of suburban planning; the highway itself was paved from curb to curb and became part of a toll road; modern gasoline filling stations and neon-lighted drive-ins began to dot its busy, tree-shaded reaches. The new real estate subdivision had a poetic name—it was a part of Harajuku-cho, which means Field Tavern Town.

The new residents of Harajuku-cho were largely substantial people, many of them commuting to jobs or businesses in Tokyo. The

"troublings" did not come from them, but—as Richi-san explained
it—could be laid at the doors of the earlier inhabitants, or, indeed,
might even be blamed on the yurei (ghosts) of the ancient highway.

The Tokaido, or East Sea Road, has been Japan's Route 1 for
more than thirteen hundred years. Along it, in full feudal pomp
and circumstance, the daimyo processions used to travel, with out-
riders crying, "Bow down! Bow down!" and samurai swords alert
to roll any head that raised before the dust of princely passage had
settled. All was high drama and colorful spectacle for the feudal
lords, but there was a drab side too: the supporting cast and the
property men were supplied by the local populace. These were the
palanquin-bearers, the porters and postboys who led the horses, the
people who carried things. They were called kumosuke, a word
now synonymous with "coolie"; they were without honor in their
lives, and without hope of improvement in the lives to come. Therefore, they begged, lied, cheated, and pilfered the packs they carried, if they had the chance.

The daimyo and samurai either killed each other off, or lived
to hand down their wealth and their honored names after the
feudal system had been abolished. But the kumosuke were forced
to keep on leeching a living from the Tokaido, which was all they
knew, through changing times. Their descendants are still on the
highway, according to Richi-san. They wash cars, wipe windshields,
and change tires; they carry trays at the drive-ins, deliver fish and
sake and charcoal to the new suburbanites, and perform all manner
of jobs and services. It is their karma—it "can't be helped, Papa-
san." And while most of them are scrupulously honest, there are
some who will still lie and cheat and steal. The Asanos should
know.

IT WAS RICHI-SAN'S BELIEF THAT JIBIKI-SAN, THE FLY-BY-NIGHT
contractor who had defrauded them, was a descendant of kumosuke, and so was the thief who stole the electric motor from their
well pump. But some of their "troublings" came from natural

causes. During the rainy season, a landslide carried away a large portion of their front yard, and dropped it into the little farming valley. It cost them a little money to have the earth restored and the steep bank in front of their house shored up against future slides, but the misfortune had its happier side. It was after the landslide that they discovered they were the fortunate owners of a toothache tree.

This was hardly more than a shrub, a species of prickly ash the Japanese call sansho, which has the botanical name of *Xanylum piperitum*. It must have been leafless during the winter of their discontent in the unfinished house, and went unnoticed under the pine trees later. But the landslide stopped at the very roots of the toothache tree, and O-jii-chan, surveying the damage, found it.

"Sansho having, oh—verree good luck, Papa-san!" Richi-san told me. "I will showing you that sansho. Can using for put on food [seasoning] and verree good for the body. And good luck. Understand, Papa-san?"

The shrub was not impressive. I looked up sansho in the dictionary. Toothache tree—an intriguing name, apparently given because the spicy leaves and berries, if chewed, might alleviate an aching tooth.

"But why is it good luck?" I asked.

Richi-san was vague on this point. "Oh, difficult, Papa-san—I cannot telling you." Then she laughed to cover embarrassment. "Maybe just crazy sinking. Maybe just *we* sinking good luck—not ozzer people."

This was a challenge to do research. It took several dictionaries and a few other reference works before I arrived at a vague understanding of what probably was a bit of whimsey and a play on words on the part of O-jii-chan. I looked up various trees in the books that essay to interpret Japan to the foreigner. They said the flowering plum is the symbol of beauty in all art and poetry, and the Asanos had planted a plum tree, already ten feet tall, in their garden. The pine represents strength—and they had sixteen pines bordering the yard. The bamboo is honored for its ability to bend before the storm without breaking, and the Japanese not only manufacture hundreds of things from the bamboo, but also eat the tender, delicious shoots. There were bamboo trees growing on the bank where the landslide had occurred.

But there was no mention of the toothache tree.

Richi-san was trying hard to help. She showed me another word in the dictionary. Sanshouo—a giant salamander, found only in Japan. This meant nothing to me until I looked up the salamander in other books. It is called sanshouo because its edible flesh has the same spicy flavor and smell as the leaves and berries of the sansho— the toothache tree. What is more pertinent, the sanshouo is credited with the very commendable ability of being able to survive even after it has been cut in half.

At this point, I began to reap the rewards of the scholar who does not give up. I wondered if the toothache tree signified hardiness— the ability to survive. O-jii-chan chuckled and nodded. He had been cut in half, economically, by Jibiki-san, the defaulting con- tractor. He had been cut in half by the landslide, which halted at the roots of the toothache tree. Signs and symbols are important to all Japanese, and now O-jii-chan, making a play on words, had decided that a sansho was a lucky thing to have in his yard.

"By the way," I said, "what about Jibiki-san? Have you found him?"

The Asanos, reluctantly, had yielded to my urging and had filed suit against Jibiki. This legal action was taken jointly with their neighbor, Komiya-san, who lived a little way down the Tokaido Highway. Komiya-san had done the plastering in the house, and Jibiki-san still owed him eighty thousand yen for that work.

When I inquired about Jibiki-san, O-jii-chan's hearty laughter filled the room. Richi-san took a Sunday pictorial from the bamboo magazine rack. "You knows chindonya, Papa-san?" she asked.

I nodded. Chindonya (the original meaning seems to have been "one-man band") are street pluggers for any product or establish- ment, sometimes with music, sometimes with banners or sandwich boards. They wear costumes. Charlie Chaplin, or Uncle Sam on stilts, frequently walks the streets of Tokyo.

"Jibiki-san where gone, I don' know," Richi-san went on. "He don' keeping busy-ness, there place. But I will showing you picture, this magazine. We sink maybe Jibiki-san now advertising some-sing, everysing. Using o-heso. Funny, Papa-san?"

"O-heso?" I asked, startled. "Honorable navel?"

"Yiss. Look, Papa-san."

It was a double-page spread on chindonya of various types, and prominently featured was an unidentified, pudgy individual with a Chaplinesque mustache. He was stripped enough to show all of a potbelly, and his navel was the center of a fascinating paint job or tattoo, thus utilizing a space the brightest young men of Madison Avenue have overlooked. If this chindonya was not the ex-contractor, Jibiki-san, it was his identical twin.

I laughed, rejoicing at the downfall of a crook, and O-jii-chan roared again. Richi-san said, "Maybe funny, but I'm verree sorree to him. Buddha never helping to him, bee-cause he don' pray to right Buddha. Maybe can't be helped. Kumosuke—I sink his family was kumosuke."

There it was again, the strong belief in hereditary traits, the evil or good handed down from generation to generation. I asked Richi-san to tell me more about kumosuke, and suggested that maybe the lawyer could locate Jibiki-san through the picture in the newspaper. But Richi-san said that a lawyer cost too much money and that they would "more praying" to Buddha. Then, while O-baa-chan knelt gracefully on the tatami to serve honorable tea, the family talked gravely among themselves for a while. I could understand very little of what they said, but I heard Komiya-san's name mentioned.

Komiya-san and his three sons, after finishing the interior plastering job on the house, had persuaded the Asanos to let him do many other things that could have waited for a more favorable period in their economy: a stone retaining wall on the street to the north, the

terrace, the traditional concrete-posted gate that was more orna-
mental than useful, and even a carport. The Asanos probably never
will own an automobile—the carport was for my use alone, and I
visited them only once or twice a week.

They had just finished paying Komiya-san for this outside work.
But Jibiki-san still owed him the eighty thousand yen for the interior job, and he couldn't find Jibiki-san. The Asanos had not hired
Komiya-san in the first place, and they had paid Jibiki-san for all
the work. But they had the finished product—the house. And now
Komiya-san, the neighbor who had been so friendly before, was
threatening to sue them for the eighty thousand yen the contractor
owed him.

"Papa-san," Richi-san began hesitantly, "we talking about kumosuke now. Jibiki-san and Komiya-san—two people, don' have good
families. Can't be helped. See, Papa-san, in old days some people
doesn't having last name, just first name. Just daimyo and samurai
having last name, and farmers and salesmen [tradesmen] cannot
keeping sword. Then Emperor changing that, and kumosuke put
on last name first time. They put on verree strong name, and sinking they can ride strong horse. But beeg *mis*-take, Papa-san—they
cannot riding strong horse! Understand, Papa-san?"

Richi-san's slaughter of the English language was always musical
and charmingly filled with the same sort of poetry found in the
talk of the American Indian: people have good hearts or bad hearts.
Their tongues are crooked. They cannot riding strong horses. I
understood. When the feudal system was abolished, retainers took
the strong names—the names of their masters. But not many of
them could match the strong accomplishments.

"How about the Asanos' name?" I asked mischievously.

Richi-san drew herself up to a proud five feet. "Oh, we having
that name maybe two hundredy fifty years! Bee-fore that, my family
name was Sugawara—Sugawara Michizane was verree strong man,
famous man. Then some kind troubling, and changee name to
Asano. I don' know why changee."

I said it was not important in today's modern, democratic, and fiercely competitive Japan, where all men are supposedly equal. The Asanos listened respectfully, and were not impressed, and I knew I was wrong. It *was* important. There was a difference, in this land where blood lines go back thousands of years. It was ancestry that gave all the Asanos their instinctive good manners, and Richi-san her beautiful grace of movement; it was the reason none of the family had a pumpkin face, like Komiya-san's wife had; it explained why Richi-san and O-baa-chan each wore a size 3½ shoe, while Komiya-san's wife had broad, splayed feet. Yet, all men are equal, and an aristocratic heritage would not help the Asanos in this new "troubling"—if Komiya-san sued.

"Give him nothing!" I advised. "Fight it. Don't pay him a cent! You have already paid Jibiki-san for that work, and you have the receipts to show it. And you didn't hire Komiya-san. Jibiki-san hired him."

Richi-san poured me some more honorable tea. "Yiss, Papa-san," she said patiently. "We will praying to Buddha about this troubling."

Komiya-san apparently thought he could frighten the Asanos into paying him, and it is just possible that he also thought that their American friend was rich—many Japanese believe that all Americans are wealthy. He did not file suit immediately, but the threat hung on all summer and autumn. Meanwhile, the Asanos continued to improve their property. They painted the house. I took two days' leave and helped them paint it. A painted house used to be rare in Japan, but now has become more common. They had their pine trees pruned and shaped in the traditional fashion, so that someday they will appear to have been sculptured by the wind.

"Papa-san?"

"Yes, Richi-san?"

"Now we having—what you speaking? Maybe insurance?"

"Insurance—yes. You mean insurance for the house?"

"Yiss, of course. Good idea, don' you? Fire and worsequake insurance, we have. And, Papa-san, don' need to money, this place.

We can fooding verree cheap! Bee-cause many sings growing on mount' and in u-oods. Just Fazzer knows zose sings, bee-cause he's countree boy. Understand, Papa-san?"

I had already tasted some of the wild delicacies O-jii-chan gathered on the mountain and in the woods. Udo, a stalk combining the best features of celery and asparagus; seri, a wild parsley; fuki, or colt's foot, and an intriguing dish which seemed to consist of tender buds, and proved to be named fukimoto, which Richi-san translated as "flower baby." He brought back yomogi (mugwort), to serve with boiled rice, and a trefoil called mitsuba. O-baa-chan stewed the onionlike bulb of the tall mountain lily, which is the flower of Kanagawa Prefecture. She made a relish of chrysanthemum petals, first boiled, then pickled in vinegar—even the blossoms were edible. O-jii-chan found large quantities of mushrooms in several varieties, some of them resembling truffles, all of them free for the gathering. Vegetables could be bought from the neighboring farms for a few cents, and fish—Totsuka is near the sea—was fresh and plentiful at low cost.

It was costing the Asano family very little to live, but also it is doubtful that they ever had more than five or ten dollars in the house at one time. Komiya-san had reiterated his threat to sue, so that it was hanging over them all that summer like a Damoclean samurai blade.

Richi-san bought a Brother knitting machine on the installment plan, and the Asano family began to turn out sweaters of hand-knitted quality, but there was no profit in this enterprise, because large mills were making the same products. She experimented in the weaving of plastic twine and tubing, and came up with a gay and colorful handbag, shaped like a dahlia blossom and lined with brocade. She called these o-fukuro—Honorable Bag, by Richi-san, and had the trademark registered. She taught O-baa-chan to make the bags, too, "bee-cause, Papa-san, she don' have job, and can working verree cheap—" and from the country she brought Etsuko-chan, a small cousin of eighteen, to live with them. A small assembly line was set in motion. Still, it took about two days of one person's time to make one honorable bag, and the family could not hope to earn more than a dollar a day for their combined effort.

But they were happily busy, and O-jii-chan was similarly occupied gathering food and working in the garden. The glory-mornings were thriving. Gourd vines climbed over the small terrace; green leaves and yellow flowers ran riot along the pergola, and even this was utilitarian. The vines produced gourds two feet long, and when they ripened they were put into water until the outer rind sloughed away and then the remaining coarse white fiber was used for back-scrubbers in the bath. Richi-san proudly told me that these would have cost fifty yen each in the stores. Their flower garden was intimate and lovely, and the house always bright with examples of ikebana, the Japanese art of flower arrangement. They rejoiced in the simple beauty of blossoms and birds and butterflies, and twice daily gave lengthy thanks to Buddha at the family altar, where the choicest selections of fruit, flowers, herbs, and berries from the toothache tree were votive offerings.

Then the blow fell. The Asanos received a court notice. Komiya-san, descendant of the kumosuke, had sued. The "troubling" had been long expected but still struck with the force of a "worsequake." The Asanos had never really understood any form of legal procedure, else they might have started earlier and shown more fight in the suit against Jibiki-san. Now they took no active countermeasures against Komiya-san's unjust claim. They were sure of only one thing, and that was that Komiya-san would be punished for his perfidy.

"Papa-san," Richi-san told me, "we was bee-fore sinking Komiya-san having good heart, helping to us. But no, *not*, Papa-san! He's kumosuke—can't be helped. He's changee face, changee heart. Now trying to catchee our house. Beeg *mis*-take, Papa-san! He will being verree sorree, bee-cause Buddha will taking care to us!"

I suggested that Buddha helps those who help themselves and keep their powder dry, and that the Asanos had better get another lawyer, quick. Richi-san said, "Don' need lawyer, and costing too muchee money. We will more praying to Buddha."

In desperation I went to my friends George Matsuyama, the former newspaperman who spoke perfect English, and Okada-san, the head of the salvage firm that had been working on the *Oneida*. Always willing to help, they met me at the Asanos' house one evening in December, when time was drawing short. Okada-san, who had some knowledge of business law, questioned the Asanos, and George gave me a running translation.

"This is worse than you thought," he said. "Richi-san can't explain the technicalities to you. But she did appear in a small claims court, on a summons. She didn't understand what it was all about, and Komiya-san's lawyer intimidated her. It seems she has put her chop on a promise to pay eighty thousand yen to Komiya-san— probably didn't know what she was signing, but it's pretty final. This was in a Kamakura court. Kamakura is not a part of Yokohama, but Totsuka is, and this house is in Totsuka. So Mr. Okada says he will look into things and see if he can't get the case thrown out of court on grounds of a lack of jurisdiction."

Okada-san's promise heartened the Asanos. O-baa-chan served dinner—tasty raw fish, mizo-shiru (bean curd soup), and the custardlike chawan-mushi. The talk turned to Japanese food, and Okada-san wanted to show me that raw squid (ika sashimi) was delicious if properly prepared. He would come again, and bring the cuttlefish. I poured George Matsuyama another drink of Scotch from the bottle I had brought for his benefit, and he sang a song about what Stanford could do to the University of California bear. We made another appointment to meet at the kokuteru house two weeks later.

Okada-san showed up at that meeting with fresh ika and his own special knife for cutting it—a formidable sheathed blade resembling a small samurai sword. He rolled up his sleeves and took charge of O-baa-chan's kitchen. He dissected the stark white cuttlefish with the skill of a surgeon, cut it in small pieces, and passed each piece very quickly through tumbling, boiling water. The result was delicious. It was very tender and had the odd flavor of corn on the cob.

Then we discussed the lawsuit. Only that morning, Komiya-san and another man had called on the Asanos. O-jii-chan, who would be polite to his worst enemy, had invited them into the house, whereupon they promptly handed him a final summons, and then went around taking an inventory of the furniture they proposed to seize by court attachment.

George studied the legal document O-jii-chan gave him, and then shook his head. "You'll have a hard time understanding this," he said. "The Yokohama District Court has upheld the lower court's judgment, probably because it was not opposed. Captain, these people are strictly out of the past! They are just too honest, and too soft. They don't realize they are living in a hard and cruel world. To you and to me, it's utterly fantastic!"

"What can they do now?" I asked.

"Probably nothing. They respect authority. The court has said it is an honorable debt, and that makes it so to them. They will have to pay before New Year's, unless Mr. Okada can persuade Komiya-san that he did a wrong thing in suing them. Okada-san is well known, and Komiya will knock his head on the tatami when he meets him. Okada-san says he will go see Komiya tonight. Maybe he can get some time for the Asanos to pay, but I'm afraid that's about all."

A COLD, DISMAL RAIN WAS FALLING. OKADA-SAN AND O-JII-CHAN took umbrellas and went down the Tokaido Highway to Komiya-san's house. There was nothing the rest of us could do but wait. George and I had more honorable tea, interspersed with a few Scotch highballs. Richi-san went into another room, where the butsudan was. She burned candles, rang a bell, and prayed.

After about an hour, the emissaries returned, wet despite the shelter of the umbrellas. They were strangely silent and sober of countenance; they needed to dry their clothing, and to be warmed by honorable tea. And when they finally talked, it was in a low, hesitant tone.

George gave me a running translation. They had been admitted to Komiya-san's house without questioning. A lot of people were coming and going there, and it was a little while before they found Komiya-san. When they did, the descendant of the kumosuke appeared dazed and ill at ease, but so excessively polite that he thanked them for coming. Okada-san told him, firmly, that he had done an evil thing in suing the Asanos for money actually owed to him by Jibiki-san—money the Asanos had already paid to Jibiki-san. He added that such a course could only lead to evil consequences.

Komiya-san burst into a sudden storm of tears and blurted that what he had done was bad, indeed. "It is true!" he sobbed. "It is true! I do not need the money now. But I cannot talk about it either. Please—do not ask me to talk about it. You see, my wife— she was in the best of health—my wife fell dead just two hours ago!"

When Richi-san and O-baa-chan heard this, their eyes filled with tears. They had seen Komiya-san's wife that very afternoon. She appeared kenkō—in perfect health.

"Oh, sorree to them!" Richi-san exclaimed. She began to weep, and then turned to me. "See, Papa-san?" she sobbed.

Like most Japanese, the Asanos collect dolls and keep them in a glass showcase. I am sure they have never heard of the practice of sticking pins into dolls representing their enemies, and that they would regard the practice as silly in the extreme. All they know is that Buddha will taking care to them, and that the wheel, in its turning, is always just.

Komiya-san knows that too, now. A few days after his wife's funeral, he came to the Asanos, humble and shaken. He attributed his wife's untimely passing to his greed, and apologized for having sued them. But, after all, he was still a descendant of the kumosuke. So he wiped away his tears and said he would settle for half— forty thousand yen.

With a little help from relatives, the Asanos could handle forty thousand yen, which is just over a hundred and ten dollars. Besides, the court had said it was an honorable debt, and all honorable debts must be "eaten up" (consumed) before New Year's.

On the night of December 31 they had their kake, a hot soup poured over noodles. This is an old Yedo custom. It is just as much a play on words as O-jii-chan used when he hailed the toothache tree as an omen of good luck. Kake means "debt," and it also means "to pour."

As midnight approached, Buddhist priests in all the temples rang out the old year by sounding their huge bronze bells a hundred and eight times. The final stroke comes just at midnight. This is to remind people that they have a hundred and eight worldly concerns —all having to do with temporal gains, and all futile.

The kokuteru house was bright on New Year's Eve. About twenty relatives from Tokyo were there, and New Year's means more to the Japanese than Christmas—although they sang some Kurisumasu songs. These included "Jinguru Beru" ("Jingle Bells") and "Howaito Kurisumasu" ("White Christmas"), along with their own soft, sweet and tender version of "Silent Night, Holy Night" ("Kiyosi Kono Yoru").

They are Buddhists. But Richi-san said to me, "Papa-san, I understand Iesu Kirisuto's [Jesus Christ's] heart. Verree good heart, Papa-san." And surely the Saviour was never paid a greater tribute.

Komiya-san heard the bells in his lonely house on the Tokaido, but nobody was there to record his thoughts.

FOURTEEN

SHADOWS ON THE STONES

ANOTHER SPRING SPLASHED ITS PASTELS ALONG THE GREEN HILLS, another summer came marching up the ancient Tokaido, and the locusts (semi) were shrilling in the pine trees. Richi-san cupped a hand behind her ear. "See, Papa-san?" she exclaimed. "This is verree strangee place—semi coming verree yearly [early]!" Then, pouring another cup of honorable tea, "Papa-san, you will pretty soon going back to States. Bee-fore going back to States, do you ant somewhere going? Good idea, don' you?"

It was a good idea. I wanted to cruise the Inland Sea, and take the Asanos to Beppu's fabled spa, and to visit tragic Hiroshima. The Asanos sent for Shinjuku Unc' to watch their house and feed their pets, and we summoned a takushi-cab to take us to Ofuna Station. The Asanos did not really want to be away from their kokuteru house, even for a few days; they walked around the garden, giving everything a last fond look. The hollyhock at the northwest corner of the house had grown to an amazing height—at least twelve feet—and was heavy with pink blossoms.

"Oh, verree good luck, Papa-san!" Richi-san exulted. "Suzukisan" (the nurseryman) "tol' me if flowers growing taller than the u-indows, it will being a verree rich house. He said."

THE EXPRESS TRAIN NAMED TSUBAME, OR THE SWALLOW, FLED southward to Osaka along the green level of the Kanto Plain, and roared through tunnels in a mountain range that hung sheer over the coast from Odawara to Atami. Then it crossed the Izu Peninsula and ran down the shore of Suruga-wan, through the tea and tangerine country. Increasing numbers of snowy white herons stood one-legged in the green rice paddies, and Masako-chan counted them. The tsuru (crane) and the kame (turtle) symbolize long life to the Japanese, and the tsuru, which mates only once in a lifetime, also represents marital felicity.

That evening, in a small Japanese inn at Osaka, everybody had a hot bath, and food was served in the biggest of our rooms. Then the family inquired the direction of Fuji-san, where the largest Nicheren Buddhist temple is located. Before going to bed, they knelt facing Fuji-san and said their prayers.

Masako-chan was convinced that she was going to be funa-yoi, which is to say seasick, aboard the steamer *Maiko Maru*, although the water of the Inland Sea was almost as smooth as a millpond. We had discovered that our party of five could travel third class, thus saving a considerable amount of yen, but could eat in the first-class dining salon. Third-class passengers ride below decks, each with a blanket, a small pillow, and allotted space equivalent to one tatami mat. They remove their shoes before stepping on the tatami section, and since nothing can be seen from that deck, they sleep, many of them removing their outer clothing to keep it from getting wrinkled. O-jii-chan and O-baa-chan had no difficulty, since they can sleep anywhere and at any time. Richi-san complained about the "dirty air," and she and Masako-chan and I went to the boat deck and enjoyed the scenery. The little steamer approached the Shikoku coast and threaded its way through a scatter of small islands, steep and picturesque, where the wind-sculptured pines ran down to the rocky beaches and were mirrored in the deep-blue water.

Here Richi-san was full of legends. She asked me if I knew the kind of small sea crab the Japanese call heike-gani, and said that many years ago there was a big battle between the retainers of the Minamoto and Taira families. "Too many ships broke, and samurai cannot swim, and was dead," she said. Their spirits became heike-gani, according to the ancient legend, and even today people cruising the Inland Sea off Shimonoseki can hear strange things at night, such as crabs bumping the side of the ship and "voices speaking, 'Help-a me! Help-a me!'" It was a sad story, Richi-san said, but it couldn't be helped. "Was war, Papa-san," she concluded.

I listened, but heard no bumpings and no voices. We disembarked that evening and took a slow train down the Shikoku coast to Matsuyama, where I had made reservations at an inn for the party. It was almost midnight when we got there, and probably we would not have found the inn at all if it had not been for a kimono-clad girl waiting at the railroad turnstile to be our gaido. She held aloft a richly embroidered purple banner bearing the inn's name in kanji, and pinned to it was a white cloth on which a strange name had been printed in ink. I had been called by this name before, in Japan, and I am still intrigued by it, and think there really should be such a title as "A. R. BIRDSWORDS."

Late next afternoon, we were aboard another steamer, called *Sakura Maru*, which glided into the harbor of Beppu and bumped the dock, and Richi-san said, "Ba-ad driver, Papa-san!" At Beppu the volcanic mountains rise high above the dreaming sea, and at first arrival one can almost feel the steamy warmth of the hot springs. Boiling water runs out everywhere; there are eight principal spas, and a number of jigoku (boiling ponds) where colored mud bubbles and jumps into the air. These are fenced off against sudden and horrible death, and, appropriately enough, are advertised with pictures of devils and scenes which might have been taken from Dante. The town is overrun with tourists, mostly

Japanese come to enjoy the baths, which are "verree good for the body."

In feudal times, a daimyo named Asano ruled Broad Island Castle and the countryside it surveyed from a flat-topped hill. This was a green and fertile delta where seven arms of a wide tidal river fanned out to meet the sea; and the rivers and the hill on which the castle had stood since 1594 made the fief easy to defend. Broad Island Town was born there of those earlier wars, taking its name from the castle. It grew and prospered, and went on to become known forever as one of the most tragic cities in history, for it died in another war, in a terrible, blinding flash, on August 6, 1945. "Broad Island," translated back into Japanese, is pronounced "Hiroshima."

The present-day Asano family and I came there overnight from Beppu, in a third Inland Sea steamer known as *Akatsuki* (Sunrise) *Maru*. Most of our fellow travelers left the ship at beautiful Miyajima—Shrine Island—just as first daylight came softly along the sea. Only a handful of passengers remained to disembark at the Hiroshima dock, and I was the only foreigner.

An American feels uneasy in Hiroshima. Neither the Asanos nor I had been there before; all of us felt qualms about what we would see. The tour of any historic battlefield interests me, but one can hardly think of Hiroshima as a battlefield. The contest was too unequal; there was no defense. It is very true that the city was a legitimate military target: in 1945, it had an Army divisional headquarters, a number of busy shipyards, and more than thirty purely military installations. It had some antiaircraft batteries, although the Americans had bombed it only lightly.

The B-29 named *Enola Gay* came over the city at 8:15 in the morning of a cloudless day, at an altitude of 29,000 feet. It opened doors to disgorge the thing it carried in its belly. The bomb fell.

It exploded 1,770 feet above the yard of a hospital.

Your world and my world, and that of the Asanos, has never been the same since that day. It never will be.

IN HIROSHIMA, OF ALL PLACES, ONE WOULD EXPECT THE POPULACE
to be ultrasensitive to any kind of loud bang, but we arrived there
to the sound of hanabi (flowers of fire) exploding over some part
of the city that was celebrating a local festival, and we soon discovered that Hiroshima is like that now—loud and gay and cheer-
ful, with an eye on business and the tourist trade. It has capitalized
on an attitude which the Japanese of other sections have described
as "Hiroshima-ism"—the perpetuation of an event which the ma-
jority of people, the victims most of all, would like to forget. It
attracts all manner of "causes," pacifist and otherwise, but most of
all it attracts the tourist. Visitors come to Hiroshima expecting to
see scars both on the landscape and on the faces of the people, and
in this they are commendably disappointed. The rubble is all gone.
The trees are young, but green and growing. The streets are broad,
and busy with commerce. (The bomb was not entirely responsible
for the wide avenues—some of them had been cleared, as firebreaks,
before it fell.) Most of the larger buildings are modern and substantial. Hiroshima is on its way to becoming one of the more beautiful
cities of Japan.

The ruined dome and broken walls of the much-photographed
Industrial Exhibition Hall were left to stand in stark memorial.
There are shadows incredibly etched on stone steps and bridge
pavement and tombstones—some of them shadows of persons who
were living until the flash came—and, of course, there are living
beings who still bear the keloid disfigurements on faces and bodies.
But the latter are not paraded for casual viewing, and time—fourteen years—has been a remarkably great healer.

THE SUNRISE MARU RUBBED THE DOCK, AND AS WE LEFT THE SHIP
we were met by a portly old gentleman who wore a cap, high-belted
trousers turned up at the bottoms, and a red armband. This lent
him an official air; I assumed that he represented a good hotel, if
not even the very efficient Japan Tourist Bureau. I could not read

the kanji on his armband, and I think the Asanos, at that point, were overwhelmed with the knowledge that they were in Hiroshima, and were watching for keloid scars everywhere they looked: they did not read it either. With the aid of two small boys, the portly gentleman manned a handcart bearing our luggage, and we followed him up the dock and across the street, and down a narrow alley where it appeared unlikely that any takushi-cab would be waiting. Just as I started asking questions, we came to a very small inn. The two urchins demanded 100 yen apiece, and then fled. The inn had no rooms at all, unless we were willing to wait a couple of hours. To the great sorrow of the portly gentleman—who probably owned the establishment—I insisted on telephoning for a takushi-cab and getting away from the harbor district, which was like waterfronts everywhere—dirty and drab. The mama-san at the inn was disappointed too, but she served us honorable tea while we were waiting. Richi-san thought she had a good heart, so I left her some money.

Hiroshima was swarming with tourists that July day, and we went a long way uptown before we finally found an inn, clean and attractive, with enough rooms. After breakfast, we summoned another takushi-cab. The only direction you need to give a Hiroshima driver is to say, "Atom bombing, please."

The place where it fell, the very center of death and destruction and history, has been well established. Science, even when working for human good, has a cold and precise way of doing things. The epicenter and hypocenter of the bomb have been scientifically and painstakingly determined by thousands of measurements of angles —principally from those shadows etched on stone. I wonder what the spirits of the old samurai, buried in Hiroshima and long at peace, would have thought about these new markings on their graves, burned suddenly across the kanji characters extolling their heroic deeds.

The Peace Museum stands here, a beautiful and modern building. Beyond it a broad esplanade forms Peace Memorial Park; it holds the Memorial Cenotaph, the Peace Memorial Cathedral and tower, a Memorial Pillar, and a huge grave mound of the bomb's unidentified victims. Along its paths, today, happy children ride their bicycles and spill over on the grass to fly kites or play baseball. They had not been born in August, 1945; they do not know. The tourists—Japanese and foreign—come this way with cameras. The surface wears no sadness, no scars.

We climbed the stairs to the second floor of the Museum. Somewhere down a long corridor, an air-raid siren wailed ominously. It ended on a thin note. Then there was an interval of silence, and organ music, soft at first, swelled triumphantly. We came to the exhibits. With a superb showmanship, they began with cave man days, with lightning and volcanoes, and the discovery of the uses of fire; they progressed to Benjamin Franklin and his kite, then to engines and ships and scientists. Einstein was there, and next to him two Japanese physicists well known in the nuclear field, Hantaro Nagaoka and Hideki Ugawa.

Then a diagram of the bomb, a description of the weather on that day when it was dropped, the blast and the shock wave, and photographic evidence of the total destruction.

The Asano family moved along this display as if hypnotized. They had fortunately been far away when it happened but they must have heard the stories of its horror many times. The stories may have been magnified and distorted out of all proportion. If they have not been, they surely will be, for epic tragedies are certain to lend themselves to legend. And yet this can never really matter, for neither tongue nor printed word will ever be able to exaggerate the horrors of Hiroshima.

In the Museum wrist watches were displayed with dials still showing the shadows burned upon them by their missing hands, forever fixing the time at sixteen minutes past eight o'clock. There was a mute array of burned and tattered clothing. A heavily retouched photograph showed the shadows of "Nine pedestrians on Yorozuyo Bridge." The ribbed skeleton of a streetcar that must have contained people less durable than their transport. Two pictures: "The former Hiroshima Castle" and "The Hiroshima Castle is no more." The hypocenter at Shima Hospital in Saiku-machi—a pitiful jumble of ruins for a place of mercy—and a photograph showing a great shroud of smoke hanging over the city as the fires spread. The pictures are not alone. Melted bottles lie here in grotesque, rubbery, fused shapes; masses of bottle caps were welded together in the twinkling of an eye, and there are bicycles, blackened and twisted, tires gone in an instant of heat surpassing that found inside the sun.

And, all the time, the air-raid siren's wail and the soft, rising, triumphant organ music. We could not tell where this was coming from, but the sound caught at the throat.

The Asanos had been silent and impassive. We moved on to the huge photographs of victims lying on blankets at Hijiyama Primary School and Honkawa Primary School. Some of them were tragically young; most of them were so horribly burned they could not have lived. The photographs were all captioned objectively and with admirable restraint: no blame was put upon anyone. But here O-baa-chan broke into sudden uncontrollable sobbing, and had to be led back to the entrance. Richi-san dabbed her eyes. O-jii-chan blew his nose loudly, and, having been a barber before he retired, was intensely interested in a series of photographs that showed the depilatory effects of radiation on several children who were rendered utterly bald.

Masako-chan was too young to be affected by any of this, other than to regard all of it with horror-widened eyes and a barrage of questions which Richi-san answered gently.

There were exhibits of stones exfoliated by the blast, and roof tiles melted, scored, and warped. Horror piled upon horror in an objective and dispassionate way, until we finally came to the exhibits showing the peaceful uses of atomic energy—a model of a nuclear-powered merchant ship yet in the future and one of a similarly propelled airliner. The sirens and the organ music were growing louder, and we turned a corner to witness a huge diorama that showed four scenes: Hiroshima before the blast (in quiet and cool green), the bombing (in red, with mushroom cloud and surface fires), the Atomic Desert after the blast, and then (with triumphant organ accompaniment) Hiroshima rising, as did the phoenix, from the rubble and the ashes.

O-baa-chan, still weeping softly, was waiting for us at the exit. We went slowly down the stairs, and nobody spoke. Just ahead of us were a young Japanese boy and girl, and they did not speak either, but they emerged into the sunlight holding hands, and their heads were high in the pride and courage of youth.

JUST OUTSIDE WAS A STRETCH OF TERRAZZO PAVEMENT, MADE WITH black pebbles. Richi-san pointed to this and said in a rather shrill voice, "Papa-san, almost looks like atom-bombed people's skin!"

I stopped where I was, all the guilt of Hiroshima upon me. "Tell me something," I said. "After seeing all that, do you hate all Americans? I would not blame you if you did."

She looked at me a moment, then gave that charming little Oriental shrug of her shoulders—a gesture that can mean a little or a lot. "Shigata ga nai!" she said in Japanese, and then translated. "Can't be helped, Papa-san. War—it was war."

Americans have heard a great deal about the Hiroshima Maidens who were sent to the United States for treatment. That project was a wonderful thing which did much to heal old wounds. But most of them know little or nothing about the important work of the Atomic Bombing Casualty Commission, which is still going on. The ABCC has headquarters in Hiroshima, in a set of quonset-type buildings which overlook the city. It painstakingly studies the effects of radiation on people who survived the blast and, in conjunction with various Japanese associations and health and welfare organizations, seeks victims who were exposed but have not yet reported for examination or treatment. When I was there some fifty American scientists and doctors were engaged in this work, along with about eight hundred Japanese. So far there has been no evidence of mutation, and that particular study will have to be carried over into the next generation. The ABCC has found increases in such ailments as cataracts and leukemia, along with making discoveries that are extremely hopeful.

It will take time. The ABCC watches and works and waits on a hill that was a soldiers' cemetery as far back as the Meji era. Behind its headquarters are memorial stones of Japanese soldiers, running into the thousands, and stacked so closely their inscriptions cannot be read. Near at hand are the graves of seven French Marines who died during some forgotten expedition to China in 1900, most probably in connection with the Boxer Rebellion. One has the feeling that they were lucky to have come to Hiroshima at an earlier date.

And in Memorial Park a stone stands in simple dignity, its inscription engraved in kanji. The guide brochures sold to tourists give the inscription as:

> Repose ye in peace,
> For the error shall never be repeated.

I like Richi-san's English translation better. It is more poetic in any language. When we were looking at the cenotaph I asked her what the inscription said, and she translated it unhesitatingly:

> This is our voice and our prayer—
> No more war.

WE WENT BACK TO OUR INN, AND I TRIED TO RECONCILE A WIDELY varying set of statistics on the Hiroshima bombing, and a lot of other things. Neither Richi-san nor her parents could help me on this, because it was all given in English. The population of Hiroshima for 1945 was listed as 255,000, but one of the more conservative brochures sold to tourists says that 260,000 people were killed by the bomb. Mayor Hamai of Hiroshima, in a radio broadcast beamed to the United States in 1949, put the death toll at more than 210,000. It has been said that there are more than 100,000 survivors who actually were in the city when the bomb exploded. If we accept the latter two figures we should have a total of 310,000 —quite a bit more than the population.

The Hiroshima Prefectural Police survey, released four months after the bombing, had supposedly exact figures: 78,150 dead, 13,983 missing, and 37,425 injured. Robert Trumbull, the *New York Times* correspondent who wrote an excellent book called *Nine Who Survived Hiroshima and Nagasaki,* puts the dead at about 60,000 and the injured at 72,000. These are round figures, but they were arrived at years after the blast and after a great deal of research. In addition to liking his amazing account of people who were atom-bombed twice, and still survived, I would accept the Trumbull figures as more accurate than any others.

Whatever the total may have been, it was, of course, too high.

I remember one evening when I was teaching the English Conversation Class in Tokyo, before I had been very long in Japan. One of the Many Cousins asked a question. Translated with the aid of Richi-san and a dictionary, it proved a difficult question, indeed. It was, "Papa-san, you think States needing to use Hiroshima bomb?"

I wished, then, that I had perfect command of the Japanese language. I told them, the best I could, that the same question probably always will be debated in our own country. I said America had every reason to believe that the Japanese would fight to the last man, and added that if the bomb actually brought about capitulation, many thousands of lives probably were saved on both sides. I tried to explain to them that conventional bombing in Tokyo and Yokohama—over a period of time—had killed more people than were lost in Hiroshima. And then it occurred to me that the latter statement really offered no justification at all.

They nodded politely, and said, "Ah, so, Papa-san," and I shall never know what they thought. I know that later I met a Japanese newspaperman who told me, "Well, it was a horrible thing. But if *we* had had it first, we certainly would have dropped it on you!"

Later I studied an Intelligence report made shortly after the U.S. Navy took over the Japanese naval base at Yokosuka and wished that I could have shown it to the Asanos. It outlined plans for the defense of the Miura Peninsula in the event the American fleet attempted to establish beachheads there. It said six Japanese naval landing forces and seventeen Army battalions were to oppose the invasion, and that among the 21,000 troops already in Yokosuka was a specially trained suicide attack unit of 1,500 men. They had forty-two midget submarines, ninety-five suicide boats, and four torpedo boats. The 71st Special Attack unit in training at nearby Kurihama had 1,000 suicide swimmers, and newly improved kami-kaze aircraft of both Oka and Kikka types were assigned.

Under "Plan of Defense," the paper said: "Defend to the last man against whatever odds. There is no provision for withdrawal."

FIFTEEN

AN OCCUPATION POSTSCRIPT

WE WERE HAVING DINNER IN THE WESTERN-STYLE LIVING ROOM OF the kokuteru house, sitting on the floor in Japanese fashion, and eating with o-hashi (chopsticks). O-baa-chan brought in a heaping platter of huge Hokkaido crab, which had been boiled, chilled, and cracked. The terebi was turned on, and a ventriloquist in a comically exaggerated military uniform performed with a Japanese version of Charlie McCarthy on his knee. This amused the Asanos very much, but I thought perhaps there might be more to the act than comedy; Socialist members of the Diet had been charging that the continued presence of American Security Forces in Japan meant that the Occupation had never actually ended. I wanted to ask the Asanos about the Occupation, but Richi-san spoke first.

"Papa-san," she asked, "what calling that kind doll?"

"A dummy," I said. "A ventriloquist's dummy."

"Verree in-ter-*est*-ing!" she said. "We calling that kind doll 'stomach doll.' "

That was interesting too, especially if the ventriloquist summons up the dummy's speech from the depths of his abdomen. I said,

"That's a very good name, Richi-san. Tell me something. What did your family think about the Occupation?"

She looked at me blankly. "More again, please, Papa-san?"

"The Occupation. How did you get along?"

"Occu—occup—I don' understand that speaking, Papa-san," she told me, and put a large piece of shellfish on my plate. "Papa-san, you like Hokkaido crab, this kind cook?"

"Yes, it's oishi—delicious. Thank you very much. But now, about the—"

"Yiss, I sink delicious. Can catching, my countree. But *not* good, Papa-san, if catching that kind crab in moonlight time, because empty. Will being empty, Fazzer tol' me. He said."

"You mean no meat? Why is that?"

"Oh, I don' know why. Maybe crab that time is changee clothes. I sink so."

"What does he do with his old clothes?"

Richi-san laughed politely behind her hand. "I don' know—maybe just throw 'em away, that moonlight time. Papa-san, you 'ant more koppu tea?"

"Thank you," I said, and had another cup of tea. They were serving hoji-ban-cha, a roasted green tea which has a distinctive flavor. "Now, about the Occupation. I mean, what did your family think of MacArthur?"

The name was magic. O-jii-chan sat straight up and said, "*Ha, ha!* Makassa!" to show he understood. Richi-san rose and wiped the ventriloquist and his stomach doll off the terebi screen. The faces of all the Asanos lighted up with comprehension, with admiration and even affection.

"Oh, Papa-san, Makassa verree fine man! Verree kindness to Japanese people!"

"Did you ever see MacArthur?"

"Oh, no, never seeing to him. But we understand he's heart. Verree good heart, Papa-san!"

Millions of Japanese still will echo those words, just as if so many "stomach dolls" were speaking, but they will utter them in all sincerity. These are the people, the masses, the middle class; those who had wealth or high government position before the capitulation might not be so kind in their judgments. A great deal of what has been written about the Occupation, to date, has been critical, and seldom complimentary. It will be a while before the definitive work can be done, because any writing of that scope will need to take into account the ultimate acceptances or rejections, by the Japanese, of the reforms the Occupation initiated—and the rejections, since the nation regained its sovereignty in 1952, have been many. On the brighter side, so have many of the ideals remained, and the Japanese, with their genius for adaptation, have shaped others more to their hearts' desire without discarding them entirely. There seems to be a basic respect for all the things the Occupation stood for when it was first established. Some of the rejections were foregone conclusions. Having regained their sovereignty, the people of Japan would naturally resent anyone's telling them how to solve their problems, for they have a great deal of national pride.

But they did not have national pride, as a people, after the surrender in 1945. Their cities were masses of smoking rubble, their fleet had been destroyed and their armies humbled. Winter was coming on, and hunger and chaos stalked the land. The Emperor, perhaps remembering that the bamboo bends before the storm without breaking, ordered his subjects to accept the "new situation" gracefully and obediently. Having been trained for a thousand years to respect authority, and conditioned by a long period of military ascendancy in their own country, the people said, "Ah, so?" and complied gracefully, indeed. So gracefully and so obediently that it has been called a dream Occupation—the very model of what any military commander could have wished it to be.

The chances are, this could have happened only in Japan. It could have been otherwise there, and almost certainly would have been much more difficult in any other country. When the Americans had landed at Yokohama in full force, they were still outnumbered, in the immediate area, by at least twenty to one. And if America had ever been occupied at all, I am sure we would still be fighting a rear-guard, never-say-die, guerrilla warfare back in the hills.

"I was working in a Japanese government office in Tokyo," the daughter of a former Japanese diplomat told me. "The head of our office called us all together to announce that American forces had landed in Yokohama, and would be in Tokyo the next day. Everybody was frightened. The office chief ordered all women employees to stay home on the following day. The American troops, he said, would rape us.

"I had lived in Vancouver, B.C., for eight years as a young girl, and had been in the States. My life ever since that time has been a conflict between bread and rice. I knew what he said was not true. I had been loyal to Japan, but now I was very excited at the prospect of seeing Americans again. I got up on a desk and made a speech. I told them it wasn't true, that the Americans would not harm anybody. I was the only woman who came to work the next day, and I was able to act as interpreter for the Americans. They were as scared as the Japanese were—they expected snipers."

The very thing that made the Occupation an outstanding success, from the military viewpoint, may well be the thing that could prevent it from proving a success when viewed in the long and cold light of history. Japanese society has always been built around groups: the family, the clan, the neighborhood organization, the zaibatsu, or business monopoly. The structure runs all the way up through the government itself; when the Emperor spoke he was speaking as High Priest, as the father to his family. Woman suffrage fits into this pattern only with difficulty; the younger generation thinks twice before it votes counter to the votes of the elders; the fixed hierarchy is the form of a thousand years, and the souls of many ancestors must be considered and consulted. In a sense, the American form of democracy which we tried to instill into the Japanese strikes at the very heart and foundation of Japanese society, because it is based on the rights and privileges and freedom of the individual. Japanese society does not recognize the individual to the same degree. Perhaps it might have been almost as easy for us to convert the Japanese to Christianity—democracy and Christianity, after all, go hand in hand—but the Christian missionaries have been working in Japan for many years and have made hardly a dent in her ninety millions of people.

I freely confess to being a Monday morning quarterback, because the Occupation had only a couple of months to run when I first went to Tokyo, and we were preparing to turn over the watch to the Japanese. But I was there not only on Monday morning, but for the rest of the week, and thus saw many of the Occupation "reforms" modified or discarded. The people who had been "purged" were being "depurged," and sometimes this mystified the Japanese, who wondered just what our policy really was. There had been excellent people in our first setup, just after the war, but many of the best were not career men, either in the military or in civil service, and after the fighting was over, they naturally wanted to go home. Their replacements were not often of similar caliber. The Occupation got off to a grand and glorious, and successful, beginning. Later it bogged down in its own mimeograph machinery— six thousand "Instructions" are supposed to have been issued to the Japanese, confusing them considerably—and in the natural processes of time enthusiasm flagged. MacArthur insisted from the beginning that no occupation should last more than three years. The Japanese Occupation lasted double that.

The early days must have been high and colorful, flushed with victory and purpose. I have talked with people who remember coming ashore in Yokosuka with the first wave of Navy and Marine Corps units. The Marines were landing, armed to the teeth and traditionally alert for snipers or kamikaze attack. They moved up the beach toward a crowd of curious Japanese, and an attractive o-josan stepped out and called in passable English, "Rieutenant, you want to make rabu? You want jig-jig?" And the lieutenant, in his best command voice, shouted, "Sergeant, take over!" And there is the story told to me by Earnest Hoberecht, United Press International vice-president for Asia, who came in with the first wave and has been there ever since. Army troops accompanying Hoberecht (I use the term advisedly, because if you know Hoberecht you know that *he* would not be accompanying the troops) were proceeding through Yokohama. Despite strict orders against looting, the soldiers were liberating a few things, such as beer—it being a hot day. A brigadier general panted out of a basement, carrying a whole keg of brew, and said, "Here, sergeant—give me a hand with this!" The sergeant retorted, "Nah-uh, general—when you're looting you're on your own!"

There was no precedent in all history for the extent of the task undertaken by the Occupation. Never before had any civilized nation attempted so thoroughly to impose its will, many of its beliefs, and in consequence much of its way of life, upon another advanced nation—from the inside. The very hope that we could do this successfully has been called naïve; the hope that it really succeeded has dimmed; the acid criticism—along with the praise for what was accomplished—will continue. And all through this, in Japan, the man Makassa shines with reputation unblemished, with character inviolate. Japan needed a strong man in those dark days of September, 1945, and he was strong. They needed a show-man, and as a showman he was superb.

"Ask your mother and father what they thought of MacArthur."

Richi-san asked. O-jii-chan cleared his throat and launched upon an animated discussion with O-baa-chan. It was obvious that they agreed: Makassa was an Honored Name second only to the August One, the Emperor. This was a generality; they got down to details, and I could understand a few scattered phrases. They were talking about food. The Japanese were hungry when the Occupation began; they were still hungry in 1946, because of the devastation and the fact that the economy could not be retooled, for peace, in such short order. There had been farm labor shortages during the war years. Transportation and distribution systems were disrupted. And a series of violent typhoons in 1945—they raised havoc with some of our ships off Okinawa—had crippled the rice crop.

"That time, after Americans coming to Japan," Richi-san began to translate, "many people verree hungry. But Fazzer and Muzzer was enough fooding. They said. Oh, not enough sungar [sugar], bee-cause nobody having sungar, that time. But enough fooding. That time, Papa-san, I was in the Tokyo, and sometimes verree hungry. Just a little rice and maybe beans, and sometimes horse meat. We was going to countree and selling kimono to farmers— I'm bee-fore telling you about that. But, Papa-san—not Makassa's fault!"

Nobody blamed Makassa. A legend persisted, and Richi-san told it to me. As a small boy MacArthur had lived in Japan, and this explained his "verree kindness to Japanese people." He had later employed a maid from Kyoto, and in consequence had ordered "no bombs for Kyoto."

Then the Asanos laughed. Richi-san said, "Oh, yiss, I remember that time—maybe *mis*-take! Fazzer speaking, Papa-san. One time was bringing from States verree strangee fooding. Some kind corn— broke the corn. Understand, Papa-san?"

"You mean cracked corn?"

"Yiss, I sink so—cracked to corn. Verree strangee. We sinking people in States never eating that kind corn, maybe just fooding to horse and cow. We don' understand what kind cook, that corn. Zo-o, verree funny!" and she went into a gale of laughter. "Bee-cause, newspapers speaking, 'hat you call—recipe? Maybe recipe. This was American kind recipe. Must using cream, and two eggs, and sungar, and must keeping long time in oven. Funny, Papa-san? Bee-cause, that time Japanese people don' have cream—never cream. Don' have eggs, don' have sungar. And oven don' have, too. Zo-o, whatcha gonna doing, that kind cook?"

"I wonder," I said. "So what did you do with the cracked corn?"

(Later I was able to look up the record on this. In March, 1946, the United States began sending food in response to MacArthur's demands, and that year Japan got 800,000 tons of wheat, peas, beans and corn. The corn, it seems, was cracked.)

"Oh," said Richi-san, "first we was trying making powder [flour] with that corn. But no good. Zo-o, many people just throw 'em away. But Makassa don' know what kind Japanese cook, Papa-san. He was verree good heart!"

I asked a Japanese newspaper friend about the cracked corn. He had been pressed into government service before the war; he composed the famous "East wind, rain" message that signaled the Pearl Harbor attack, but he told me there was something nobody knew. At the same time, Japan was in deathly fear of an attack by Russia, and if this appeared about to take place, another code message would be sent, saying, "North wind, snow."

Perhaps it is too bad the latter dispatch never went out. It would have changed the course of history.

"Sure, I remember that cracked corn shipment!" he said. "It probably came about as a result of the U.S. farm surplus. The Japanese press was ordered to print that silly recipe about cream and eggs and ovens—that was one of the inconsistent things about the Occupation. It was supposed to be teaching us democracy, including a free press, but MacArthur's people controlled the press very closely. They would not allow any story to be printed criticizing MacArthur or the Occupation."

"And the cracked corn?" I prompted.

"Oh, yes. Well, I was glad to get it. I was hungry, and, after all, it was food. Anyway, it probably wasn't MacArthur's doings—somebody on his staff and somebody back in Washington must have been responsible. We couldn't get to MacArthur, in those days, to ask him about anything. He was too well insulated. It would have been about as easy, for the Japanese newspapermen, to interview God Himself."

Other Asanos had a harder time during the early days of the Occupation. Shinjuku Aunt and Unc', whose home had been burned in the fire raids, were living in a shack made of packing cases, with four children, when winter came on, and the supply of bean paste they had hoarded was running out. There was no heat: everything that would burn, in Shinjuku, had already been burned. They suffered more in the first year after the war than they had during the conflict, but they nurtured no bitterness toward America. The Japanese militarists had brought these trials upon them, and the militarists were either dead or in Sugami Prison. The suffering was shikata na gai—a "can't be helped" thing. They viewed it, along with the atomic bombing of Hiroshima, as a natural disaster, such as the Great Earthquake and Fire of 1923. . . .

A STRANGE PEOPLE, INDEED, FOR THERE WERE MILLIONS LIKE THE Asanos, like Shinjuku Aunt and Unc', accepting what the radio voices told them, repeating it like "stomach dolls," believing it until it became true, being serene under hardships, and trying very earnestly to understand the new democracy. The intellectuals, the thinkers, the statesmen and journalists—none of these had voice during the Occupation, and many of them have not been heard from since. Someday a Japanese will write a critical analysis of that great undertaking. When he does, we can scarcely expect it to be objective, and perhaps it will be colored with extreme opinion. But it will not be dull.

I should expect any such report to point up confusion, and to say that the Occupation should have been turned over to civil authority immediately after its inception, since we professed the intention of stamping out, forever, militarism in Japan. I should be disappointed if it failed to deal with such undemocratic practices as press censorship and special privileges for the Americans at the very time when we were preaching democracy. No doubt it will make much of our seemingly strange about-face on armaments—in one breath we were insisting that the Japanese renounce armed strength forever and in the next (after the Korean War) we did our utmost to persuade them to build up their armed forces, so they could take over their own defense and provide us a bulwark in the Far East.

Most of all, I should like to read about Japanese reactions to our policy of coddling American military personnel to the extent that dependents began to be funneled into Japan by the thousands, at a time when every tsubo of living space was precious, a time when the best houses in Tokyo and other places were commandeered for the American families, and put "off limits" to the Japanese. We were the conquerors—yes. We could and did do it. Never mind the supermarkets of commissaries and post exchanges that enabled our people to overlive the Japanese in every regard—the Japanese were not accustomed to such luxuries, and we were. The best hotels were turned into military billets. The best railway cars, and even the elevators—both often half empty—were also "off limits" to what the Occupation called "indigenous personnel," and so were the lowly and ubiquitous jeeps.

I submit that "personnel" means a body of persons employed in a service, particularly a public service: it does not mean the people of a nation at large, but the off-limits rules were so applied. The word "indigenous" to me has always suggested a vegetable, rather than a human being. I must admit, however, that the Occupation Forces were on occasion consistent. In at least one directive, or instruction, they referred to the "indigenous population of the United States."

Being an indigenous American, and a Texan full of the old rebellious spirit, I shall always feel that the Occupation decreed unworthy things. One of these was the removal of the antiquated guns from the old battleship *Mikasa*, Admiral Togo's flagship in the Russo-Japanese War. A military Occupation is a Big Thing, and an order such as this one must have resulted from literal interpretation and from thinking at a very low level. It was the equivalent, say, of an order to strip the gun deck of *Old Ironsides*—give or take a few decades in the development of naval weapons—and of about equal military importance. The *Mikasa* was already solidly and helplessly enshrined in concrete at Yokosuka, and her main battery was as effective as the cannon at Fort Ticonderoga. But she meant something to the Japanese. Now the guns are gone, and cannot be found. They, along with the *Mikasa* herself, were nothing but a shinboru—a symbol—but they happened to be a symbol against Soviet Russia, and that sort of thing will be important to us for some time to come. The entire procedure was silly, but the end results are not. In this period of cold war, when Japan is our hope and our fortress in the Far East, we need both strength *and* symbols against Soviet Russia.

MacArthur was quoted by an Associated Press man as saying he had only two advisers—George Washington and Abraham Lincoln. It would have been well if he had remembered Commodore Matthew Calbraith Perry, who first brought America to the Japanese islands back in 1853, because the Occupation was an extension of Perry. After a very short time it ceased being the military guard and became the teacher.

At that point, it should have stopped being military. But there were too many people eagerly seeking decorations, or—at least—good fitness reports. There was too much "completed staff work"— a thing by which the military sets great store, and something that greatly increases paper work. It would appear that during the Occupation staff work was sometimes completed before the fact.

What the Japanese had at first accepted in good faith became questionable: the Americans were advocating one thing and living another. Just when we could have become the teacher there was a lack of respect for our teaching, and it became migi kara hidari e nukeru, or "in the right ear, and out the left."

But paradoxical things came to pass. Just as the Japanese were losing faith in democratic processes, Makassa, their idol, was fired. This had a strange effect. It proved that the United States was not really a militaristic power. It showed that anybody was vulnerable. It proved that civil administration of the military really worked.

It was not a bad thing, after the initial shock wore off in Japan.

The people said, "Ah, so? Can't be helped." They carried on with Rijuei, which is what they called General Ridgway, and they liked him. But it wasn't the same. Nothing was ever the same after Makassa.

SIXTEEN

NEVER SPEAK SAYONARA . . .

MY ORDERS HAD COME IN THE SPRING, BEFORE WE TOOK THE IN-
land Sea trip and saw Hiroshima. They gave me three months to
prepare for the move to Norfolk, Virginia, where I was to join the
staff of NATO's Supreme Allied Commander Atlantic. I told the
Asanos about it, and they said, "Ah, so?" and looked solemn and
sad for a moment, and then Richi-san said gently, "I understand,
Papa-san—I know that kind sing. Navy—is Navy busy-ness. Can't
be helped. Papa-san coming back to Japan someday?"

"I hope so. I must come back to visit Japan and see how you are
getting along."

"Oh, we will fine!* But if you can coming back to see us, we
will verree happy. I sink you will being happy, bee-cause can seeing
your family again. And new job *beeg* job, I sink so. NATO is many
countries, Papa-san?"

"Yes. International—kokusai. To fight Communism."

* Since this was written, letters from Richi-san reveal that the Asanos
have finally started their "small busy-ness." It is a coffee shop, built over the
carport at the northwest corner of the kokuteru house, and is named Yama-
no-yuri, or the Mountain Lily. May it enjoy all of Buddha's blessings!

Richi-san said that Communists were verree ba-ad, and translated for the family. Then she said, "Papa-san, we will going to the ship that day. But you don' speaking sayonara, and we don' speak too. Just you speaking maybe 'So long! Be careful!' and we speaking 'Mata dozo, Papa-san be careful.' Understand?"

I said I understood. Mata dozo means 'Please come again.' And sayonara is at once perhaps the most beautiful word in the Japanese language and the most difficult to pronounce when the time comes to say it. (I once wrote this sentiment into a short farewell address for a tough and rugged-looking admiral who was leaving Japan, and I think he did not read the speech until he was on the podium. When he reached that line, his glasses misted over, his voice broke, and he had to grope his way to his seat.) So I was glad not to have to speak sayonara.

"Papa-san 'ant more koppu tea?" asked Richi-san.

I drank the tea, and reflected on what she called "Navy busy-ness," or orders. My naval career had been a broken sort of thing, rather accidental; it came about as a result of the fortunes of war, and I had only a total of eighteen years of active duty, man and boy. I had remained in Japan much longer than the Navy had left me in any other place. It occurred to me, as I looked back down the years since I first enlisted in the Navy, in Texas, as an apprentice seaman, that I had been around fairly well for someone not engaged in aviation duties. West Coast, East Coast, Panama, West Indies, Iceland, Newfoundland, Hawaii, Noumea, Espíritu Santo, Guadalcanal, Bougainville, and other South Pacific islands with feathered palms and bloodstained coral sands; Alaska, the Aleutians, Japan, Korea, Formosa, the Philippines, Okinawa, and a few other way points. I remembered a sound that is the same no matter where you hear it: the slap-slap of lanyards on a tall pole where the American Flag is flying in the wind. There is no other sound like this one, and it sustains you when you sit safe and secure at an administrative desk and can hear it outside. It comes to mean something, because so long as the Flag ripples high in the wind, even though it be an alien wind, all is well. . . .

And then I reflected that of all the places I had been, outside my own beloved homeland, I had liked Japan best.

Why? It wasn't the climate. You can find any kind of climate in Japan, because the islands run roughly from 46° North to 30° South, and are both caressed by the gentle Japanese Current and buffeted by Siberian winds, and because the altitude runs all the way from sea level to towering, snow-clad mountains. But that part of Japan in which I spent most of my time is somewhat similar, in its weathers, to the weathers of Washington, D.C., for which I hold no violent affection.

It wasn't the scenery. Japan has extremes of scenery, from sea-coast to mountains, and it is always beautifully green. But New England matches the greenness and does pretty well with the sea-scapes. The Rockies of Colorado are more magnificent; the Pacific Northwest is outstanding, and the Southwestern deserts show colors that cannot be found anywhere else. America has the added advantage of spaciousness and cleanliness that cannot be matched in crowded Japan.

It could not have been the customs or the food or the dress of the people, interesting and exotic though all of them may be. The customs are charming but alien; the food is the same, and an American would not wish to eat it every day. Taken en masse, the people wear drab enough clothing except on those special occasions, festival days, when the female population—young and old—blossoms forth in its Number One kimono. Then the land is as lovely as a land of flowers in which each individual bloom is beautiful, colorful, and gay. There should be more such o-matsuri. Tokyo is very fashion conscious, and quickly susceptible to Parisian trends—the sack had its regrettable season on the Ginza—and many an o-josan is entirely beautiful in Western clothes. On the other hand, there are probably millions who should never, never attempt to squeeze their short feet into spike-heeled shoes, because their once graceful and provocative walk becomes a painful parody.

My liking for Japan—my genuine affection for the country—had to come from the people themselves. In this fondness I admit to having made a limited approach. I know only one family well; the Asanos may not be representative. But they were worthy of observation and—what is infinitely more important—they were eminently worthy of warm and enduring friendship.

The Japanese are an ordered people, long accustomed to regimented patterns despite the new democratic freedoms. By and large, they respect the law, whatever it may be. They are an excessively energetic people. Even a crew of laborers repairing a streetcar track goes at its task as if it had to be accomplished before the next trolley comes along, and that is a refreshing sight. In all my time in Japan I never saw a man or boy leaning against a building; the people are always in motion. They are a people who cherish cleanliness and tidiness against great odds. They are a people to be pitied—and helped—because the land has run out and there is no place for them to go. The population increases explosively despite birth-control campaigns and legalized abortions; mountains and seashores squeeze the seventeen per cent arable land that must feed the added millions, and only by harvesting the sea can Japan eat.

A people to admire, because with so little they have done so much. Above all, a people to keep on our side, in wars of the future, cold or hot. Because Japan occupies the same geographical position, in relation to Asia, that England holds in reference to Europe. Japan is our landing and launching platform in the Far East. It is our industrial and technological arsenal, and our pool of manpower with the know-how and the skill to produce the useful implements of peace or the wasteful weapons of war.

When and if Red China ever overtakes Japan in that regard, with its overpowering weight of millions, then—if China is still Red—may God help us all. . . .

EARLY ON AN AUGUST MORNING I WAS DRIVEN TO HANEDA AIRPORT, which is Tokyo's International. The Asano family, accompanied by a couple of their neighbors who knew me, arrived late by separate automobile; I was about ready to board the Military Air Transport Service plane before they came.

We did not speak sayonara. I shook O-jii-chan's hand, and gave O-baa-chan a hug that startled her out of her serenity, and kissed both Richi-san and Masako-chan. I waved my hand airily and said, "So long—see you again!" and they said, "Mata dozo, Papa-san— sank you verree much! See you again!"

Then I walked out to the big four-engined aircraft and got aboard. I could see them, standing small against the airport building, until we had taxied away. When we came down the runway for the take-off, speed blurred everything; I could not be sure that they were still there, waving to me.

It was a hot, bright morning, and the heat haze had not yet come over the Kanto Plain. A few clouds were making up, but Fuji-san still towered in cool blue majesty in the southwestern sky, the symbol of all things Japanese.

Spoken or not, this was sayonara. . . .

Oshimai—The Honorable End

Set in 11/13 Fairfield
Format by Jacqueline Wilsdon
Manufactured by American Book—Stratford Press
Published by HARPER & BROTHERS, New York